I Was Born
Under The Hotel End.

Quentin Jones

Quentin Jones

This book is dedicated to the
memory of Mary Clark.

First published in 1996
by **Quentin Jones.**
PO Box 702,
Olney,
Bucks,
MK46 5FH.

ISBN 0 9529117 0 1

Printed in Great Britain by
Avalon Print, Moulton Park, Northampton, England.

CONTENTS

THE AUTHOR

Quentin Jones was born in Wharley End, Bedfordshire in 1966. At the age of two he moved the short distance to Olney in Buckinghamshire with his parents. Apart from nine months when he lived in Wollaston, Northants, Quentin has lived in Olney ever since.

He was educated at Olney County First and Middle schools before attending Ousedale Comprehensive in Newport Pagnell. He readily admits that he spent very little time studying for his 'O'-levels because he was either playing cricket (for Olney Town and Northants County Colts) or watching football! The only books studied were Wisden Cricketers Almanack, Playfair Cricket Annuals and Rothmans Football Yearbooks.

Quentin is the longest contributor to the Northampton Town Fanzine, "WALOC - What A Load Of Cobblers!" and has a regular column in the Northampton "Chronicle & Echo". He is married to Sharron and his hobbies include reading, walking and visiting Whitby in North Yorkshire.

PREFACE

This book covers the five seasons of Northampton Town between 1991/2 - 1995/6. Without a doubt these were some of the most dramatic times that any Football League club has ever been through. I and many others continued to support the Cobblers through these dark times. The following pages chronicle these five long seasons through my eyes, a self confessed die hard supporter.

I have split most of the chapters into seasons. The second chapter about season 1991/2 covers very few events on the pitch. This sums that season up entirely. Events off the pitch totally dominated proceedings.

In writing this book there are individuals I must thank. My good friend John Whelan for the picture on the front cover. John and his wife Alison must also be thanked for their kind friendship, especially when things were tough for me. When I first started this book I had a design for a front cover in my mind. When I showed a very rough design to Simon Black, he went away and with the aid of various computers and scanners came up trumps. Two very big thankyous to my wife Sharron and my mum Joan who both had the awful task of proof reading the text. Without their help this book would never have gone ahead. I must mention Brian Lomax, Chairman of the Northampton Town Supporters Trust and Director of Northampton Town. He will never know how grateful I am to him for his patience, trust and openness. Unfortunately, much of what we would like to have printed has been omitted for legal reasons. My final thanks goes to Pete Norton for supplying three photographs which have been used in the book. Pete went to a great deal of time and trouble to get these pictures to me. I was humbled by his kindness.

As I was putting the finishing touches to this book a friend of mine popped round to see me. With a look of disbelief on his face he told me the news that Alan Shearer had been sold by Blackburn Rovers to Newcastle United for £15 million. The very same day I was having lunch with a Leyton Orient fan. The conversation was about the Shearer transfer, a world record. We were both disgusted by it. Both our respective clubs had come close to extinction in the 90s. I hope that when you read the following chapters, you will realise why we were so sickened by the Shearer deal.

Why am I Obsessed?

I have to confess it myself. I am obsessed with Northampton Town Football Club. So how did it all start? What makes me travel up to Burnley on a Tuesday night to watch a game of football, knowing that I have to start a twelve hour shift at 06:45 the next morning in Milton Keynes? Why do I do it? Why do I follow a club that always seems to be in the lowest division of the Football League and in its one hundred year history has only been in the top flight for one season? What made me continue to support this club that, for three years in the early 1990s, was a stone's throw away from either extinction or being relegated to the non-league? Why bother, especially when you know that what you have witnessed has been at its best mediocre, at its worst utter garbage.

I suppose in some sort of strange perverse way, following a club that is unlikely to ever take the footballing world by storm is a sort of pleasure. But it is more than that. I reckon I have become used to following a side that, in the time I have been supporting them, the highest they have been is top of the old third division for a few days in 1988 until we got well and truly hammered one evening up at Brammall Lane. And yes, before you ask, I was there. I could jack it all in now, right this very minute. Tomorrow I could go to the Grosvenor Centre in Northampton, buy a Manchester United, Liverpool or Arsenal shirt and claim to be one of their supporters. Immediately, success would be guaranteed, dates at Wembley, trips to Europe and million pound players. If I did that though how could I live with myself? What sort of pseudo snob would I be? My team is Northampton Town. End of story. If someone wants to pooh pooh me about this then fine. That's their problem. I have now supported the Cobblers for well over twenty years. I have become used to the snide remarks, the wind-ups, the mickey-takes, the off-the-cuff comments. When people make comments like these to me, and it is often, it is usually accompanied with laughter and smirks. It does not rattle me anymore. I became used to it a long, long time ago.

I became football crazy very early on in life and it was my Dad who took me to see my first ever league game. It was 13 April 1974, Northampton Town v Peterborough United. I later found out that this game was to be remembered more for events that went on after the game. Peterborough United are the Cobblers' local rivals and on this day so-called supporters of both clubs clashed in Abington Park. Many years later several individuals I know still recall that day clearly. Some of the incidents occurring in Abington Park were so violent that the area actually resembled a battle field. The scenes of violence witnessed have gone down in local history and the incident is now known as "The Battle of Abington Park". Fortunately my Dad and I missed all of this. Although memories are obviously sketchy I still remember bits of the day, like being in the Spion Kop with all the Peterborough United fans. For the record, Cobblers lost 1-0. The next day the match was featured on Anglia Television's "Match of the Week". I said to my friends;

"I was at that game."

Needless to say I was hooked.

As a result of my initiation at the County Ground it was not long before I was hassling Dad to take me to another game at Northampton. Never in his wildest dreams did he ever think for one minute what the consequences of taking me to see one game at the County Ground would be. Even now he says,

"I never thought it would go this far."

He still shakes his head in disbelief when I tell him that I will be going down to Exeter on a Tuesday night. Well as far as I am concerned, he only has himself to blame. It was he that also took me to my first ever away match at Brentford. That was the day when I discovered that the Cobblers' away kit in those days was blue and what the taste of beer was like! My Dad took me into a bar under the main stand at Griffin Park and bought me my very first ale! I was only about eight years short of the legal age for consuming alcoholic beverages!

Now, some twenty plus years later I'm still as obsessed as ever. Most things pale into insignificance in comparison to Northampton Town. Work comes into that bracket. When I left school in 1982, two weeks into my 'A'-levels, I started working for the Coop. (It is surprising how many people I know used to work for the Coop.) Not a bad job but I had to work Saturday mornings. Although this was a bind it still meant that I could get to home games. By the mid-eighties I have to confess that my loyalty to the Cobblers was not as good as it could have been. For a couple of years I missed too many games. I don't really know why this was. It could have been part of the growing up process. I know that when I finished work on Saturday lunch times all I wanted to do was get home and put my feet up. Sometimes I could just not face finishing work, jumping on the bus and going straight off to Northampton and then haring up the Wellingborough Road to get to the County Ground on time. Now of course I regret it. I cannot turn the clock back and change things. I know I have missed historic occasions. Because of my apathy I missed one of the biggest games in recent times for the Cobblers. It is a day that shall only be mentioned once in these pages. The date was 19 March 1985. I don't want to dwell too much on what I missed and how I was personally to blame. All I shall say was that the Cobblers played Chester City at home that night. Nine hundred and forty-two fans turned up. It was the first and only time that less than a thousand fans turned up to see a Northampton home game. I still feel guilty. If I had been present then there would have been nine hundred and forty-three. Another fifty or so and there would have been a thousand.

When I suddenly found my old enthusiasm returning, my employer decided to extend the working hours of the shop. This of course meant Saturday afternoons. This coincided with the time when Graham Carr took over as manager of Northampton. In a very short space of time he had plucked some unknown names from the non-league and Cobblers were suddenly on a roll. In 1986/7 Carr's side took the Fourth Division by storm. Crowds started flocking back up Abington Avenue as players, who have now gone down in Northampton Town folklore, walked away with the championship. Trevor Morley, Richard Hill, Eddie McGoldrick, Dave Gilbert and Keith McPherson to mention a few, were just too hot to handle. When Cobblers won the Fourth Division in 1986/7 they set all sorts of records. Over a hundred league goals were scored; ninety-nine points were secured; in all competitions, five players, Hill, Gilbert, Morley, Benjamin and Chard had goal tallies reaching double figures. Hill scored an incredible twenty-nine league goals. It was a great time. The County Ground bulged full to the seams as crowds flocked back. For the only time that I can ever remember I used to turn up at the County Ground and expect the Cobblers to hammer the opposition, and they usually did! By 1987 I was working every Saturday and hating every moment of it. I was missing far too much football. My games were restricted to evenings, bank holidays and leave. Northampton paid the price for success. Many big clubs had been trailing various individuals in the squad. Being a relatively small club Cobblers felt they had to sell to survive. In my opinion this proved to be a huge mistake. If a player wanted to go then fair enough but if the club had been courageous like Tranmere Rovers and managed to hold on to their quality players, then things could have turned out a lot different. Within two years of winning the title many of the stars had left. Names that will remain in the memories of Cobblers' fans forever. Richard Hill to Watford. Trevor Morley to Manchester City. Eddie McGoldrick to Crystal Palace and the Republic of Ireland. Dave Gilbert to Grimsby.

By the end of the 1989/90 season Northampton had been relegated. They had been in the old Third Division for just three seasons. After the final game of that season, Graham Carr packed his bags along with two of the last three survivors from the 1986/7 season, Russell Wilcox and Keith McPherson. When Cobblers played their last game of that season, at Rotherham, the Club already knew that they were relegated. Although the game was completely meaningless from the Cobblers' point of view, I still felt a severe loyalty to the cause and made the trip to South Yorkshire. Relegation from the old Third Division was nearly the beginning of the end for the Cobblers. The following season Theo Foley was appointed manager. From where I was standing it looked like he had been given a directive to go flat out for promotion. No holds barred. He assembled a large squad, many of them had been on second and third division wages. That would have been all well and good if the Cobblers had gone straight up to the top of the division. Crowds would have again flocked up Abington Avenue like they had four years previous. They didn't though and within two years the club had its back to the wall. Surprisingly the Rotherham game was and still is only the second time I have experienced relegation with Northampton!

I have experienced practically every emotion whilst following the Cobblers. Many are very painful, others pure magic. I have made numerous friends through the Club. I have seen places that I would otherwise never have seen. As a direct result of following the Cobblers I could probably compile an extensive documentation on the country's fish and chip shops! There are moments that I have hated but when I look back I feel that because I have experienced such lows, I am a stronger person. Sitting on a coach outside Crawley's ground with all their supporters walking past jeering at us after they had stuffed us 4-2 in the cup was a truly awful moment! Two Tuesday evening 5-0 away hidings at Burnley and Scunthorpe were horrific. Hearing Dave Martin's arm break in an away game at Gillingham (who he later went on to play for) was one of the worst injuries I have seen (or heard). Thankfully there was no gore but the break echoed around the ground. It is all part of the experience.

Dave Martin, seconds after breaking his arm at Gillingham

There have of course been good times. One of my earliest memories was in 1976 when Cobblers played Bournemouth at home. Heading towards half-time Cobblers were leading 1-0. Then in the eight minutes before half-time Cobblers scored five goals. The ball just kept hitting the back of the net. The entire 1986/7 season was like a fantasy. Richard Hill eating up entire midfields. Keith McPherson winning practically every tackle. Eddie McGoldrick flying down the wing. The class of Trevor Morley. The County Ground packed to the seams week in, week out. Will I ever see a side like that again? Then there was the day in 1988 when Cobblers caused a huge shock in the FA Cup when they put out Coventry City. These moments rarely happen.

Moving out of the County Ground into Sixfields was terrific. In the space of four days we went from having probably the worst ground in the league to having the best ground in the division. A ground to be proud of. A ground that really turned out to be a miracle. I could rattle on and on about the good and bad times but at the end of the day I'm really glad I've witnessed it all.

In 1991 I started working for a large financial institution. I had to work shifts. This meant that I again had to work most weekends. In the summer of 1992 I calculated that I had worked twelve out of fifteen weekends. Family life, social life, football and cricket went out of the window. In October 1992 I was made redundant. It came as a blessing in disguise. From that moment on I was determined never to work shifts and Saturday afternoons again. I've done my fair share.

Society is changing and so is the face of football. Money is becoming more and more influential. Players are being paid thousands of pounds every week. The top ones are being paid more in a week than I earn in a year! Transfers are hitting seven and eight million pounds for top players. FIFA was rumoured to want to make the size of goals bigger. TV channels can dictate the days and times of kick-offs, however unreasonable. The Premier League players now wear silly squad numbers on their shirts. Enough is enough as far as I am concerned. Leave the game alone. Football is worth far more than money. Football clubs may be businesses but they are also part of the community. If a club is top of the league or on a good cup run then the town can often reflect that. Whatever happens in the years to come one thing will never change. I will still have my claret and white scarf on.

In writing this book I have found out about many practices that used to go on (and almost certainly still do) in the world of football. I do not wish to write about those. Thankfully, my club, Northampton Town has cleaned up its act. As far as I know they were the first league club to have not one, but two democratically elected supporters representatives on the board of directors. This of course has not passed without problems and personality clashes. What a lot of clubs have got to remember is that it does not matter who owns the club, who owns shares in it or who is a director. At the end of the day the supporters are the club. Without people turning up week in, week out and fans buying season tickets in the middle of the summer, many clubs would fold.

This book is centred around Northampton Town Football Club. For most of the years I have supported them there has been little to cheer about. Yes I suppose I have become used to the struggle. Mark my word though. I would change the struggle for some success. I have a little dream. One day I hope to see Northampton climb out of Division Three at long last, build on success and in time end up in the Premier League. The success could be crowned by a trip into Europe and a Sixfields that is two tiered, packed to the rafters every week. I know this is a dream. There is little chance it will ever happen because money and lots of it is needed to even get a sniff at top flight football now. Money talks big in the Premier League. I loved every minute that tiny, unfashionable Wimbledon have fought amongst the big boys. I would love it even more if Cobblers were up there scrapping away.

Cobblers 1986/87

1991/1992

Aldershot

There was a unique atmosphere at the Recreation Ground Aldershot on that Saturday in early March 1992. Just under one thousand four hundred people had gathered to witness what could have been history in the making. Two clubs, Aldershot, one of the very few sides which I hold any affection for, and my beloved Northampton had a Fourth Division fixture to fulfil just days before they could both be wound up in the High Court because of their enormous debts. There was more than a strong possibility that within two weeks of this game one, if not both clubs, could be history and the result of the afternoon's proceedings would be null and void. This was the case when on the afternoon of 26 March 1992, Aldershot Football Club's finances, or rather lack of them, had gone too far down the road and it was announced that the club would be wound up the next day. It was a miracle that Aldershot had survived so long and incredibly, as Cobblers were due in court on March 11th, it could have been them, not Aldershot, who were wound up first.

The trip down to Hampshire had started in mid-morning when my mate Fred and I were picked up by the Supporters Club coach at Newport Pagnell Services and settled down for the trip down the motorway. There are some grounds I really hate going to, Lincoln and Notts County for instance. In the late eighties/early nineties when you got to those grounds you were herded into an away end and your view of the game was dramatically reduced by being positioned in a far flung corner surrounded by fencing. Aldershot revives good memories. Even in a 5-1 drubbing there, we witnessed a fantastic own goal volleyed in by Paul Wilson and an Aldershot forward rounding Peter Gleasure and missing an open goal from five yards out. At Aldershot, goals and entertainment were always guaranteed. In fact I would go as far as saying that the Recreation Ground at Aldershot was my favourite ground in the entire league.

On arrival at Aldershot signs that the East/West cold war had ended became apparent. The huge complex of multi-storey army living apartments were in the process of being demolished with huge piles of concrete lying where they had once stood. We pulled up at a pub not far from the Recreation Ground, which in my opinion is the main focal point of the town. Being the home of the British Army is irrelevant. If it has got a football league club there, which Aldershot had then, then in my book that's far more important.

After supping a couple of pints of draught Bass I met up with Fred and we wandered down to the main entrance. The turnstiles at Aldershot are like bus stops. I hope they never pull them down. If they do then they should be saved and put in a museum. Like red telephone boxes which have been replaced by these awful Americanised kiosk affairs, the turnstiles at Aldershot are a part of British heritage. Just behind the main stand on a terrapin hut which served as the club shop, sorry words like "The Shots Must Not Die" had been painted.

Collecting buckets were going round. Like many hard core Northampton supporters at the time there were many Aldershot fans who were going to great efforts to try and save their club. Reading their programme there was obvious unrest at Aldershot but nothing like the scale there was at Northampton. Outwardly there did not seem to be the hostility towards their Chairman as there did towards the extremely unpopular Northampton Chairman Michael McRitchie. It was noticeable that when the two clubs met at the County Ground in January, 1992, the Aldershot Chairman Mr Gladwell left the stand and went into the Spion Kop to mingle with the fans that had travelled up from Hampshire. I just could not have imagined Mr McRitchie doing that! The police would have had a riot on their hands!

At kick-off, the terraces were a lot barer than I had previously seen at Aldershot. It seemed that most of their supporters had called it a day feeling that things had gone far enough. The game commenced and with twenty-seven minutes gone, a speculative shot from thirty yards by Shots' Tony Joyce somehow managed to beat Barry Richardson and they were one up. A few Aldershot fans started either singing,

"One team in Northants!"

or

"One team in North Hants!"

I don't know which it was but it certainly went down well with the Cobblers' fans who started chanting,

"Aldershot, Aldershot......"

This started off a remarkable chain of events which must be unique in recent times. Both sets of supporters were singing along together and applauding each other. Cobblers then equalised and a claret and white hat was thrown over the fencing into the Shots section. Return fire was exchanged with a blue and red hat thrown back. Scarves were also swapped. At half-time two of their supporters came through with a collection bucket. At this point I asked a policeman why the supporters were still being kept apart by the locked gate in the fencing.

"It's not up to me to make that decision. It's up to a senior officer", came the reply.

The gate remained locked but as half-time ended four of their fans were let through to stand with us. Twenty seconds into the second half Aidy Thorpe made it 2-1 to the Cobblers. It is the only time in my life that I have ever felt any sympathy for opposing supporters when Cobblers have scored! Full credit to those four Aldershot fans. They must have felt as sick as dogs then. With Thorpe running rings around the Aldershot defence the match finished 4-1 to the Cobblers. One might have thought that I would have felt elated after such an impressive victory away from home but I didn't. I felt doom and the strong feeling that I would not be coming back to Aldershot, not to see football anyway. Just over two weeks later I was proved right.

Forty-eight hours after the Shots were wound up, two of their supporters managed to get on the Radio 5 606 programme. They were obviously shell shocked and were pleading for no other league teams to go the same way. I could not give a monkey's if there was no more Old Trafford, but it made me angry that the Recreation Ground was wiped off the map without a flicker of emotion from certain quarters. The second of the Aldershot supporters on the radio was the Assistant Secretary of their Supporters club. He was overwhelmed by the generosity of the lower division clubs' supporters who had tried to help the Shots. He especially thanked the Cardiff City and Northampton Town supporters. It appeared that none of the larger clubs, apart from Swindon Town seemed to have offered any help. On 28 March Northampton played Cardiff City at the County Ground. Both sets of supporters gave Aldershot a standing ovation. Whatever came out of those desperate times at Aldershot it brought a lot of lower division supporters closer.

Aldershot never saw the 1991/ 92 season out. Cobblers' 4-1 win at the Recreation Ground never happened. The Football League expunged all of Aldershot's league records for that season. However, Aldershot did reform as Aldershot Town and the following season ended up in the Beazer Homes Division Three playing in front of crowds of well over two thousand. Unheard of in that grade of football. I still miss my once a season trip down to that part of Hampshire.

A Club in Crisis

Just before the start of the 1991/2 season, life as a Northampton Town supporter seemed to be its usual self. Then in August and September 1991, reports started to surface that all was far from well at Northampton Town Football Club. The reports centred around reliable information that the Club was heavily in debt and that it was struggling to pay players properly. Several supporters, including Rob Marshall, editor of the Club's Fanzine, were worried that the Club and its Chairman, Michael McRitchie, were saying that everything was all right and there was nothing to worry about. In early December a group of supporters from the fanzine (Rob Marshall, Brian Lomax, Denise Brown and Gerry Fallon) were so worried by what they were hearing that they got together and discussed what could be done. Rob Marshall suggested a public meeting and asked Brian for his guidance. Brian was a Director of a charity that helped local homeless people and he also had previous experience in the political arena. It was decided to hold the public meeting as soon as possible. The proposed format was that the supporters of Northampton Town would be invited to come along and Club officials would be asked to attend and give truthful information regarding the current state of the Club. It was thought, that with the right sort of information, the fans could be involved in helping the Club deal with its problems and to establish some form of partnership. It was felt that for many years, apart from the short time when Derek Banks was Chairman, communication between the Club and its supporters had been very poor.

Because of this informal meeting amongst the four, the first public meeting was called for the first week in January 1992. At this very early stage in proceedings, Brian Lomax and his colleagues had very little, if any idea what would come out of the meeting and had no doubt that the Club's officials would come. Unfortunately in a very short space of time, the Club announced in the press that they would not be attending and could see no value in it being held. They said that if they wanted a public meeting then they would have called one themselves. At this stage in late December 1991, Mr Lomax and his colleagues assumed that with the Club not attending the meeting, it would be a complete flop. This would be a shame as a room at the Coop Exeter Rooms on the Kettering Road, which could hold two hundred and fifty people, had been hired and they very much doubted whether one hundred would turn up.

On the afternoon of 2 January 1992, just hours before the public meeting was to be held, Brian Lomax arrived back from Cheshire to receive a message that the Club had now decided to attend the public meeting. The damage though had already been done. It was too late for many supporters to know this. (I personally know many people who would have attended if Northampton Town had originally stated that they would be present.) Brian Lomax was asked to chair the public meeting and everyone present will never forget that night. Despite the Club's original statement that they would not attend, some six hundred supporters packed into the Exeter Rooms. I arrived there after finishing a twelve hour shift in Milton Keynes. It was great to see that for once apathy had not won. At the start of the meeting, Brian received a written proposal from a life long supporter, for an appeal on behalf of the club. At this stage in proceedings, nobody had any idea that the Northampton Town Supporters Trust would be formed. The atmosphere in the Exeter Rooms was incredible. There were so many supporters present that the hall could not cope with the volume. All the seats were taken and people were crammed into the back and sides of the hall. Even the entrance was filled with fans desperate to get in.

Along with Brian Lomax and Rob Marshall at the front of the hall was the then manager of the Club Theo Foley and the new Commercial Manager Paul Clarke. Also present were two members of the local council. Questions started raining in from the floor. One though kept being asked of Mr Clarke,

"How much debt is Northampton Town in?"

Answers did not appear to be very forthcoming from the platform. Looking back on that night one cannot blame Paul Clarke for his vagueness. He was very new to the job and many people believed that he genuinely had no idea of the true figure involved. The one person who would have had the answer to this question, and for the sake of the Club and all its loyal supporters should have been present that night, was Michael McRitchie, Chairman of Northampton Town Football Club. He had sent his apologies due to sickness. It was later found out that Mr McRitchie had been at a dinner dance in Kenilworth.

Midway through the meeting a former Director, Martin Pell made a statement from the floor. As a shareholder he had access to the accounts. By his calculations he reckoned that the Club was a staggering £940,000 in the red. In response to this Paul Clarke then stated that, despite not knowing the exact figure, £940,000 was probably close to the exact amount. This bombshell stunned many people, including myself. It was then that most supporters realised the true enormity of the Club's predicament. Being an average supporter with an average type of job, with an ordinary, nothing special type of salary, £940,000 was a figure so large that I could hardly comprehend it. For such a small, unfashionable Third Division club I was trying to figure out how on earth Northampton Town was ever going to recover from this.

Theo Foley stated that he believed the most pressing problem was not long term but short term. I suppose he had a point. The more the average supporter found out about the Club, the worse it got. Northampton Town long term was not looking to be a problem at all because the short term was so bad that there appeared to be no light at the end of the tunnel.

During the meeting a proposal was put forward that a trust should be formed. The proposal was overwhelmingly voted in and so the Northampton Town Supporters Trust was born. At the meeting it was felt that there should be an independent fund accountable to the supporters. It was also felt that at that time in early January 1992, no money should be handed over to the football club until their accounts were shown. There was an overwhelming feeling at that meeting that dealing with Michael McRitchie was like sleeping on a bed of stinging nettles. It was beginning to become a stressful time for everyone connected with the Club and at that time there appeared to be two Northampton Towns. One was a bankrupt club, whose players never knew whether they were going to be paid or not and which had creditors threatening court action at any moment. The other was a club steeped in tradition who, for one season in the 60s, had competed in the top league in the country against the mighty Arsenals of this world. A club who, for decades, had its name on the pools coupon and had produced quality players like Dave Bowen, Phil Neal and more recently Trevor Morley and Eddie McGoldrick. This Northampton Town had some of the most loyal fans to be found anywhere who would go to almost any length to save their club and who were screaming out for some democracy and most of all honesty.

Towards the end of the meeting I found myself deep in thought. The Club was well and truly going to the wall. It had been alleged that the Cobblers were losing £7000 a week. Foley had announced at the meeting that Tony Adcock had been sold to Peterborough for £60,000. (It later emerged that Bobby Barnes had also gone to Peterborough in this deal.) He then stated that the money left after the transfer should keep the Club going for about two weeks! I looked in my diary. Saturday 11 January, weather permitting, Northampton Town v York City at home. The Club needed an immediate cash injection. Obviously there was no way on this earth that £940,000 was going to materialise out of thin air. Many individuals present at that meeting had also stated that they were unwilling to help financially until the accounts were shown and the true enormity of the situation was known. If Foley reckoned £60,000 would keep the Club running for another two weeks I had an idea of how to inject anything up to £50,000 straightaway. As Foley had said, at this stage the problem was short term. There appeared to be no long term future at the Cobblers.

I attracted Rob Marshall's attention on the platform. At that time I had known Rob pretty well for about four years as I contributed articles for his fanzine. The meeting was drawing to an end but Rob had given me the thumbs up so I knew I would have a minute or two to address the meeting before it ended. As I was called up to have my say I have to confess I was very nervous. Never before in my life had I addressed so many people. As I arrived at the front of the hall I pulled my diary out of my pocket. I wanted my little piece to be remembered. Not from an egotistical point but from the message I was trying to get across. I noticed that the hand holding my diary was shaking like a leaf. I quickly put my diary away! I knew what my first line was going to be. I turned to look at the members of the press who were sitting in the corner to my right. I said,

"This is a direct appeal to the members of the Press."

Immediately I could see their attention had been drawn. As I started to speak I could see them writing away. My appeal went along these lines. On January 11, Cobblers were playing York City at home. If people really cared about the future of the Club then they should turn up at the County Ground next Saturday. If the Club could get an attendance of say ten thousand then £50, 000 would go straight into the Club. If Foley reckoned £60,000 would keep things ticking over for two weeks then a bumper crowd against York would keep things going just that bit longer. The chances of getting ten thousand people for the York game were very slim. In 1986 the official gate went over ten thousand for the Boxing Day fixture with Cardiff City. At that time though Northampton Town were top of Division Four, the side was the best I have ever seen playing in claret and white and Derek Banks was a popular Chairman. When I finished my short speech the hall erupted in applause. I state again. I did not do this for me. I much prefer to put my thoughts down in black and white. I certainly did not enjoy facing six hundred people and making a short speech.

In the days after the public meeting, the Club was initially helpful towards the newly formed Supporters Trust which was due to be legally constituted on 10 January. Paul Clarke had agreed that the inaugural meeting of the Trust could be held in the Directors' Lounge at the County Ground. On Wednesday 8 January, Mr McRitchie announced at a press conference that he would have nothing to do with the Trust. All co-operation was withdrawn and the Trust would not be allowed to collect in the ground at the forthcoming match with York City on the Saturday. He also refused facilities for the Trust to hold their inaugural meeting in the Directors' Lounge at the County Ground. Brian Lomax thought that there must have been a misunderstanding, so the following day, Thursday 9 January, he rang the Club and asked to speak to Mr McRitchie. He said that the Trust wanted to work with him and not against him. Paul Clarke arranged a meeting for the next morning at 11:30.

That morning, Brian Lomax arrived on time. With him was Bill Cowie who ran the St James Supporters Club (known as the Jimmies End). They were kept waiting for half an hour before being ushered into a room. Surprisingly they were not to be the only people there. Also present were Mr McRitchie, Jeff Welch from BBC Radio Northampton and Jeremy Casey, a journalist from the Northampton Herald & Post. On entering the room the meeting got off to a less than auspicious start as Mr Lomax introduced himself to the Chairman saying,

"My name is Brian Lomax and I'm pleased to meet you."

Mr McRitchie replied,

"I wish I could say the same."

Let's just say that the meeting did not go well. Eventually it seemed to Brian Lomax to be futile and a waste of time. He had not gone there to be insulted, he had gone there on behalf of a number of faithful supporters who followed the side home and away, week in, week out. He told Mr McRitchie this. The meeting closed and Mr McRitchie and Brian were interviewed by the journalists in front of each other. Brian left the room upset and shocked.

That evening in the Abington Park Hotel, the Trust adopted a constitution for a legal status and its officers were elected. January 10 was to prove a historic moment for Northampton Town Football Club as the Supporters Trust legally came into existence.

Crisis, What Crisis?

The financial situation was so bad that the Club was apparently living from week to week not knowing whether the next would bring oblivion. Some supporters from other clubs such as Bristol City, Wolves and Tranmere Rovers had been through similar experiences, but many other supporters, who I hope are reading this, have not and will not experience what the supporters of Northampton Town were going through early in 1992. It is not pleasant. Football becomes an obsession, your club a religion. The thought of life without the Cobblers does not bear thinking about. It would leave a massive void. In early 1992 Cobblers' fans turned up to every game not knowing whether it would be the last one they would ever witness. Most attention seemed to be focused off the pitch where rumours of alleged unpaid wages and bouncing cheques were circulating.

In the opening days of 1992 I decided to keep a diary. On January 2 the public meeting took place at the Exeter Rooms. As I have already explained, I did something that I never thought I would ever do. I stood up and addressed six hundred people. This is briefly what I did in the days after the public meeting. It was not much. What could I do? I was working twelve hour shifts in Milton Keynes. I did not live in Northampton. I had very limited access to the Northampton press and media. Who the hell was Quentin Jones anyway! I felt I had to do something though, even with my limited resources and time. I decided to attack the press and get as much coverage about the York City game as possible.

Thursday, 2, January, 1992.
After the meeting had ended in the Exeter Rooms I made my way over to the area of the room where the press were situated. I sought out the reporter from the Chronicle & Echo and urged him to give as much coverage as possible for a bumper gate at the York game the following Saturday. He said that he could not guarantee headlines every night on the Cobblers. He then started to ask questions about me. I stated to him that I was not interested in publicising myself. Who the hell was interested in me for crying out loud! The future of the club was very doubtful. I wanted that put into the headlines. I wanted as many people as possible to know that it was vital for them to get to the County Ground the following Saturday so that the Club's short term future could hopefully continue for the time being. That was what I wanted in the spotlight, not details about me. I understood at the time though, and went privately on record as saying that there was very little chance of getting ten thousand people through the turnstiles for the York game. As far as I knew, York City did not have a large away following. The Cobblers were not taking the footballing world by storm as they did in 1986/7. If six thousand supporters turned up that would be brilliant. Any supporters who turned up that would otherwise not have done would be a bonus.

Friday 3 January 1992.
I got home late the previous night. I again found myself at work at 06:45 to start my twelve hour shift. At lunchtime my boss came on site to tell me that he had heard about the public meeting on the radio. He did not know what station it had

been on. That though did not really matter. At least people were aware of what was happening and how desperate the situation had become. I rang my local newsagents and asked them to put a Chronicle & Echo by for me. I would pick it up in the morning. I also arranged for "About Anglia" to be recorded.

Saturday 4 January 1992.
Cobblers had no game. Typical. I was off shift for the weekend and there was no football! I got up early and walked down to the newsagents to collect my Chronicle & Echo. The Exeter Rooms meeting had hit the front page. Not only this but there were further reports on four other inside pages. From a personal point of view I was interested to see the comment on page six. There was a headline stating that more fans were needed through the turnstiles. The plea for the York game had been mentioned. I hoped that the game would get further coverage during the next week. I had a few plans up my sleeve for that! The first of these came at five past six when I switched on Radio 5 to listen to Danny Baker's football phone in. At twenty past six after I thought that the initial rush would be over, I rang up that now famous phone number. I explained what I was ringing about (the financial crisis at the Cobblers). They took my name and number saying that they would try to get me on and hopefully ring me back. Unfortunately I never got the call and did not get on to the show. Northampton did get a mention though. A Kettering fan on his way back from their exit in the cup at Blackburn managed to rub the Cobblers' noses in it!

Sunday 5 January 1992.
I got hold of the video of the Friday night edition of "About Anglia". One of the lead stories was about the public meeting. Brian Lomax who had chaired the meeting was interviewed along with fanzine editor, Rob Marshall. I sat down and planned my assault on the press. I also wrote to Theo Foley. I asked him to mention the plea for supporters in any interviews he gave before the game against York City. (I don't know how true it was, but I was told that Foley had contacted the Saint & Greavsie show and they had mentioned it at the end of their programme before the York game.)

Monday 6 January 1992.
I wrote to fanzine editor Rob Marshall. As he was one of the people who had called the meeting and was on the platform, I asked if it would be possible for me to be a representative of the Trust when talking to members of the press.

Tuesday 7 January 1992.
I wrote to the editor of the Chronicle & Echo. I hoped that it would be published on the letters page. I was not overly confident though. The newspaper's letter page was overwhelmed with mail about the Cobblers' present position. The letter was short, sweet and straight to the point appealing for fans for the York game.

Wednesday 8 January 1992.
A slightly different form of attack. I rang Anglia Television in Northampton. They told me to contact the main news centre in Norwich. I called Norwich and spoke

to their news desk before being put through to the sports desk. I suddenly found myself talking to one of the presenters, Richard Henwood. I ended up briefly explaining who I was, what I was representing and why. He seemed pretty interested in what I had to say. His ears certainly seemed to prick up when I mentioned that I had contacted Theo Foley! I felt that there may be a mention of the appeal for supporters on their Friday night sports round up.

Thursday 9 January 1992.
I rang the BBC in Norwich. I got through to their sports department and ended up speaking to someone, I don't know who though. Their presenter, Mark Liggins was in a meeting. The man whom I spoke to said that he would get back to me. He never did. I reckoned Cobblers would be lucky to get much of a mention from BBC East the following night.

Friday 10 January 1992.
After I had finished my twelve hour shift I made my way straight over to Northampton to attend the official forming of the Trust. Originally the meeting was to be held at the County Ground but Mr McRitchie had refused to let the Trust use the Club's facilities even though they were trying to help. The meeting was transferred to the Abington Park Hotel at the eleventh hour. When I arrived I heard that Anglia TV had mentioned the appeal for supporters, excellent. I also heard that somebody had printed some posters advertising the appeal for fans for the York game. By all accounts the town had been swamped with them. Whoever did this, whoever you are, it was a fantastic idea. The Trust was formed and an executive committee was elected. I finally arrived home at 22:30. I had just finished a sixteen hour day. I wondered how many fans would turn up the following day?

Saturday 11 January 1992.
D Day. I arrived at the County Ground and put my loose change in a collection bucket. As I wandered along the back of the Hotel End I saw Brian Lomax, the newly elected Chairman of the Trust. He walked past me looking very angry. Perhaps that should not read very angry. He was more than that. Mr Lomax looked like he was nearly at boiling point! Mr McRitchie had apparently thrown the collectors out of the Hotel End entrance. As kick-off approached there was a larger crowd than usual. The Hotel End looked pretty full. It was obvious that for many people it was their first game in a long time. At half-time the official gate was given as three thousand three hundred and fifty-five. Exactly the same as the Blackpool home game earlier in the season. I could see people around me looking at the terraces shaking their heads. Unless many fans' eyes were deceiving them there appeared to be more fans than that in the County Ground. Was the appeal for supporters a success? I personally believe that the gate had doubled, so yes it was. For the record the game ended 2-2 with Steve Terry and Bobby Barnes scoring for the Cobblers.

I may not be a millionaire who could have pumped my money into Northampton

Town FC. However, I reckon I did my bit. I do not want to single myself out here. There are many more people who did a lot more than I did. Two days after the York game Mr McRitchie went on a live phone in on BBC Radio Northampton. I and thousands of other people listened in absolute disbelief at some of the things he said. From where I was standing what little credibility he had left vanished out of the window.

Desperate Times.

At the inaugural meeting of the Trust it was decided that Brian Lomax, who had been voted in as Chairman, would contact the Football League by phone and inform them of its existence. This was done early the following week when he spoke to Mike Foster, the League's assistant secretary. Brian wished to establish the Trust's credentials as a voice of the supporters. If there was any discussion at league level about the future of the Club, then the Trust wished to be involved. He asked the League to put this in writing.

As it emerged that Northampton Town had failed to pay their players in November and December 1991, the Trust decided to contact the PFA. Once again this task was carried out by Brian Lomax and he spoke to Mick McGuire. He told Mr McGuire about the formation of the Trust and why it had been formed separate from the Club. The supporters wanted the Trust money handled independently and not given directly to Northampton Town FC. Mr McGuire then said,

"Gordon Taylor has come to exactly the same conclusion."

Other matters were discussed and both parties resolved to keep in touch.

In the weeks after the Trust was formed, it was stated in certain quarters that the Trust was a method of ex-directors trying to get back on the board! At that time in early January 1992, nothing could have been further from the truth. Only one ex-director, Martin Church had joined the Trust. The Trust's new executive committee was busy drawing up its own business plan to save the Club. They were highly doubtful whether any big money man would come in for the Club or even if it would be desirable. This was hardly surprising. Mr Lomax and his colleagues had only one goal, to make sure that Northampton Town FC was in good hands and run on a sound basis. It wanted a democratic approach and at that time believed that a committee was the only safeguard for the Club. However, being realistic, they knew that supporters on their own could not produce enough money coupled with gate receipts to run a football league club. An astonishing £12,000 had been raised in the first two months of the Trust's existence. There was no way this amount of money could ever be maintained. The Club had assembled a much too large squad whose wage bill was crippling.

After the public meeting, the Trust worked very hard behind the scenes. They realised the importance of involving the business community and a number of approaches were made. The Trust soon knew that if control of the Club was to change then a number of people and businesses had contributions to make. They were, however, unwilling to donate into the Club whilst Mr McRitchie was still in control or to give it to the Trust if they did not succeed in their aims. There were a number of private understandings with individuals who were prepared to invest in a McRitchie free club and back the Trust's business plan. The Trust was able to obtain a list of the names and addresses of most of the Club's creditors from a source close to the Cobblers. Two officers of the Trust contacted all the creditors and they seemed willing to view the Trust's plan favourably.

The plan was to offer them shares at a face value of £5 each, to the extent of the amount owed to them. They could then, at a later stage, sell these shares back to the Club for cash when it was in a position to buy them. There would be an arrangement that they could only sell them back to the Club, nobody else. The creditors were quite willing to go along with this. At this stage, if a winding up order had been granted and a receiver appointed to take over the running of the Club, the Trust could approach them with its own business plan. The receiver would then have time to receive any other business plans and to call a meeting of the creditors and it would then be their decision which one they would support. The Trust knew that even if another plan was forthcoming, the majority of the creditors would support the Trust. So as February approached, it began to get more and more tense at the County Ground. Life and league fixtures somehow continued at Northampton Town who were due in the County Court on March 11.

On 11 March 1992 events took a backward step for the Trust and their business plan. The judge at the County Court adjourned the case against Northampton Town. Again the Trust had been working very hard behind the scenes. They had continued negotiations with the Football League who had agreed to meet the Trust within twenty-four hours if the winding up petition was granted. They wished to discuss the future of the Club and to consider how to resolve it. The Trust had found out that there were strict conditions under which people forming a new company can take over the affairs of a Football League Club when it is liquidated. Every pressure is on the Football League to negotiate so that the League fixtures can be completed. With the winding up petition going to court on March 11, it was hoped that a new Board for the Club would soon be in place with the Football League's blessing. The judge had adjourned for eight weeks which would have taken the case out beyond the end of the season. That meant that the Football League would be under no pressure to negotiate with the Trust as the fixtures would be complete. Brian Lomax believed that the League would rather have a prosperous Conference side come into the League than a club like Northampton who were now highly unlikely to survive and on the point of extinction. The adjournment weakened the position of the Trust and its business plan.

The adjournment had taken place because Mr McRitchie had put forward a rescue package. At the hearing a provision was made by the judge that the creditors must be kept informed on a weekly basis of negotiations by Mr McRitchie on behalf of his rescue package. Very soon it became clear that his negotiations had broken down. This meant that, if they wanted, the creditors could bring their case back to court in seven days, sooner than the eight weeks the judge had imposed. By this time the Club's position was so bad that this looked like the only way it could survive.

There had been two parts to Mr McRitchie rescue package. One concerned a construction company who, if they won the contract for the new stadium, would give £500,000 to the Club. The other part involved two ex-directors. Two days after the court hearing, the Council announced that it was putting the entire new community stadium scheme on ice until further notice. There would be no dealings with any firms of contractors and the name of the construction company Mr McRitchie had linked with his rescue package was mentioned. That meant that part one of Mr McRitchie's rescue package fell through only forty-eight hours after the hearing.

Brian Lomax desperately hoped, for the sake of the Club and all its supporters, that the creditors would bring the case back to court for late March. Indications at that time were that one of the creditors, Abbeyfield Press was seeking to do this because of the stadium proposal collapsing. As March was ending though, things were still at a standstill. Every kick of every game involving the Cobblers during this period seemed to be overshadowed by events going on off the park. The Trust's view was that the most likely outcome at that moment was for Northampton Town FC to be wound up and the Football League deeming it beyond recall.

That would leave just one other option. The forming of a new club with the Supporters Trust money and starting off in the United Counties League. This now looked on the cards. If at the end of the 1991/2 season Mr McRitchie was still at the Club and the winding up petition was granted then that would be that. Apart from the floodlights the Club had no assets. They did not own their ground. The Trust just could not have taken the Club on.

By this time Brian Lomax personally believed that, however sad and unwanted it would be, the best thing that could happen to Northampton Town would be for them to go under. They could then start out on a decent basis and build up strength again in the non-league as AFC Newport had done. He had been told by The Cockerill Trust, who owned the County Ground, that if the Trust formed a new club then it would have automatic access to the County Ground. Although the Supporters Trust was only two months old it was already highly respected in many important places from the Football League to local businesses. It started off with one objective but in a very short space of time found out all the nasty, dirty things that had been going on at the Club.

As April approached the Trust knew of seven or eight people who were interested in putting £15,000 into the Club and getting three thousand shares back in return. This offer of one share per £5 donated would also be open to the Supporters Club, the Borough Council and the Trust. This would provide initial funding and capital to immediately pay off creditors who, for obvious reasons, could not accept shares. i.e. the Inland Revenue, Customs & Excise and the Northants Police. The capital would also cover running costs between May and August when income was greatly reduced. The other creditors would be offered this new issue of shares which would be floated to the public. People could then be shareholders, however large or small.

On the Brink.

The future of Northampton Town Football Club took an enormous jolt in late March 1992. Mr McRitchie forestalled any further action from the creditors by approaching a firm of insolvency experts, Pannell Kerr Forster in Birmingham. He asked them to take over the running of the Club. For the first few days this was an unofficial arrangement between themselves and Mr McRitchie. The Supporters Trust had anticipated this move and had spoken to the administrator earlier that week. Also that week, the Trust had had a meeting with several ex-directors which had taken place on March 30. Present from the Trust were Brian Lomax, Barry Collins, Roy Parker and Phil Frost. The ex-directors present were Barry Stonhill, Mark Deane and Martin Church. It was agreed that the two parties should enter into a partnership to save the Club subject to the approval of the Trust executive committee.

On the evening of Tuesday 31 March the executive committee of the Trust held an emergency meeting which was interrupted midway through as the Cobblers were playing Rochdale at the County Ground! It was a long meeting. The Trust needed to establish that, if they went into any partnership with the ex-directors, it would have equal and not just token representation. Some of the Trust were worried that the ex-directors may see them merely as a glorified supporters club. The agreement that finally came out of the meeting was a resolution for a full and equal partnership.

On Thursday 2 April the order of administration was obtained at The High Court in Birmingham. This meant that the administrator took over the affairs of the Club. The Cobblers were not answerable to Mr McRitchie but to the Court. The administrator then invited the ex-directors and the Trust to attend a meeting the following day at 11:00 at the offices of Pannell Kerr Forster.

Brian Lomax, Phil Frost, Mark Deane and Martin Church turned up the next day, Friday 3 April, at the administrator's office. On arrival they discovered that Mr and Mrs McRitchie had already been there for an hour. They also discovered that at nine o'clock that very morning, a member of the administrative staff had been to the County Ground. On arriving there, this person issued dismissal notices with instant effect to nine players and the management team of Theo Foley, Joe Kiernan and Billy Best. Also to go was striker Christian McClean who was a non-contract player. One of the players released was long serving goalkeeper, Peter Gleasure. Out of all the tragic dismissals, this was the one, certainly for me, which really stank. Gleasure had set all sorts of records in his Northampton career and was a year short of his testimonial. Many loyal supporters were far from happy with the way he had been treated on the playing front. (Foley had dropped him.) Some supporters did not rate Gleasure, but for many others he was a cult figure. He was also the last surviving member of the famous 1986/7 championship winning side.

The Trust were very worried by the dismissals. Their concern was that supporters would think that it had in some way been involved in this move. On several occasions Mr Lomax and the Trust had to make the following statement.

"The Trust had no knowledge of the dismissals prior to the event and had no part in the selection of who should or should not be kept. There had been rumours that some sort of quick action like this was going to be taken. These rumours had not been confirmed and it was a shock to learn that the Cobblers had lost twelve members of staff."

On the morning of April 3 the administrator, Barry Ward, told the group of four that he would like them to meet with Mr and Mrs McRitchie, without him being present, to decide who would run the affairs of the Club along with him. Mr Ward said he would accept a majority decision on this and he would then form an interim Board of Directors. He was clearly giving a signal that if the four were to stand firm and say Mr McRitchie had to go then that would be the decision made. The only person who could now hire and fire directors was the administrator.

Lomax, Deane, Church and Frost then met with Mr and Mrs McRitchie. Mr McRitchie resigned with a certain amount of dignity. He wished the four the best for the future. He said that the administrator had done the hard work by dismissing the staff and putting the budget back into balance. At this point Mr Ward rejoined them and Mr and Mrs McRitchie left. Mr Ward had already drawn up an agenda for a board meeting. He said that he proposed to form a Board of five directors, four ex-directors and one Trust member. The two Trust members there told the administrator that this was not acceptable to the Trust committee because it appeared to be a token representation. Mr Ward stated that he did not want a large board and that he would set an absolute maximum of six. It was agreed that four ex-directors and two Trust members would form the new Board. Events were happening so quickly! The administrator was informed that the Trust would have to hold an election to decide who would be their Board representatives. Mr Ward accepted this but stated that he had to be notified by the following Wednesday.

As the two Trust members left the administrator's office one thing was certain.

With Mr Ward allowing two elected Supporters Trust members on to the Board of Directors of a Football League Club, history had been made. Initially the order of administration was for four months. That was soon extended to twelve months. This meant that all the Club's debts were frozen for that period of time. The Club had a year to show that it could trade at a profit.

Barnet Away 4.4.92.

Amidst all this turmoil, one thing had almost been forgotten. The very next day Northampton had a League fixture to fulfil at Underhill, Barnet. One of the experienced players who had been retained, Phil Chard, had agreed to become player/manager. It was a complete mystery as to who he was going to play.

This was and still is one of the weirdest games I have ever experienced. The utter relief and joy on the faces of hundreds of Cobblers' fans will stick in the mind forever. At the end of the day, the result was pretty meaningless. For 99.9% of Cobblers' fans the biggest match of the season had been won the previous day when Mr McRitchie's control of Northampton Town had disappeared. As kick-off approached fans were singing, dancing and for the first time in many months, smiles could be seen on their faces. I bumped into Brian Lomax, who by then I knew pretty well as a friend, outside the gents! You could see the adrenaline flowing through him. He was a very satisfied man but we both knew that there was still a very long way to go. For the time being though, we both revelled in the news that it was the administrator who was Chairman of our football club.

As so many players had been released it was a job to know who would be playing in claret and white. New player/manager Phil Chard came back into the side after a long lay off with a serious injury. Into the side along with the players who had survived the axe came youth team players Danny Kiernan, Sean Parker, Martin Aldridge and Rickie Bulzis. Not surprisingly, Barnet came away with a comfortable 3-0 victory. That did not matter to the travelling supporters though. When the final whistle sounded it was as if Northampton had just secured promotion. Many of the Cobblers' players seemed bewildered by events. Two players though, Steve Terry and Terry Angus came over to the Cobblers' supporters and insisted on shaking as many of the outstretched hands as possible. Steve Terry was saying,
"God bless you" on every handshake. I suppose thinking back on things it must have been a very strange time for him and his colleagues who still had jobs with Northampton Town. Just like you and I they have mortgages and bills to pay. They were lucky enough still to have a job!

The Season Must Go On.

On April 15 the Trust decided to hold another public meeting. The occasion was also used to launch the Cobblers Help Line, a major fund raising exercise. Before this, questions were heard from the floor. The main question referred to the "hit list" of dismissed staff. Where had it originated from and who was behind it? Brian Lomax was able, once again, to assure the membership that the Trust had had absolutely nothing to do with the sackings and had had no idea how the list had been arrived at. Concern was also expressed at the position of Mr McRitchie and how much control he still had? Some people were also concerned that at the end of the administration order he would be back on the scene.

Also on the platform that evening was Mark Deane. Before the Help Line was launched Mr Deane stated that he had attended a League meeting the previous day. He indicated that Northampton Town's name was mud with other League clubs. He also said that an alleged "hit list" existed as the League were planning to trim the number of clubs from seventy-one to sixty-six. This was going to happen by natural wastage. Unfortunately, these revelations distracted most people away from the Help Line, including the press who were again present that evening. Many people left that meeting thinking that the Club was going to fold regardless. Thankfully the Help Line proved to be a success and helped the Club financially.

Another very important announcement regarding the future of the Cobblers happened on 29 April. At an executive committee meeting of the Trust Councillor O'Leary went out of his way to say that the proposal for the new stadium had not been shelved. It was still going ahead but delays had occurred in clearing refuse from the site. It would definitely be built as a community stadium and the Cobblers would be the tenants. These comments were unsolicited. At last there seemed to be a Council which was committed to the new stadium. Incredibly, in spite of their still very unpredictable position, Northampton Town looked like having a new stadium, possibly in 1994.

At this time in late April 1992, the new Board was concentrating on the future. In the previous month it had become obvious that many bills had remained unpaid from the preceding three years. Mr Ward told them not to worry themselves with past finances as they were frozen. Pannell Kerr Forster had the task of drawing up a list of all debts and creditors. All remaining wages were up-to-date. This continued through the summer. The Trust made no more contact with the PFA which was obliged to take action on behalf of those members who had been dismissed on April 3. Neither the Trust nor the Board had any brief to talk to the PFA.

Before the end of the season more youngsters were given a chance at league level. Lee Colkin, Mark Parsons and Jimmie Benton. Against all the odds the scratch mixture of remaining first teamers and youth managed to win the last game of the season away at Hereford. Northampton Town finished the 1991/2 season in sixteenth place in Division Four, eighty-sixth in the league.

As the summer of 1992 approached, the fans of Northampton Town had hardly had time to draw breath. The previous five months had been nothing like anyone had ever experienced before. The Supporters Trust had ended up with two of its elected members on the Board of Directors. In the years to come the Trust continued as a high profile part of the Club. It was to have good times and bad times. Now and again it would end up with egg on its face, just like all other organisations. Throughout though, its chairman Brain Lomax, in my opinion, has always conducted himself with great dignity. As he is first and foremost a supporter, he would (and at the time of writing still does) get approached on the terraces, not always in the most friendly of manners. Being a director, many fans would see him as a someone to vent their feelings and anger at. This will not be the last you will hear about the Supporters Trust in this book. In the final chapter I will bring you up-to-date.

1992/1993

The Conference Beckons

Somehow, against all the odds, Northampton Town Football Club had survived the 1991/2 season in tact, but only just. To this day much of the football world, including many supporters of the Club, will never know how close the Cobblers were to joining Aldershot in oblivion. Without wanting to sound too dramatic it was as though all depended on the toss of a coin. Fortunately, someone called correctly!

There was an enormous price to be paid for survival. The cost was on the playing front. After Mr McRitchie had finally left the administrator's office in April 1992, the administrator Mr Ward, in saving the Club, had sacked nine players and three management staff. This proved to be one of the most damaging events ever to happen in the history of the Cobblers. The heart of Northampton Town had been ripped out. Looking back though, there was no other option open to the administrator. His action was like giving mouth to mouth resuscitation and then severing an artery. The sackings would have a knock on effect for years to come.

In spite of all that had happened, Northampton started the 1992/3 season with an away game at Gillingham. Unfortunately I was playing cricket and missed the game, but after all that had gone on in the previous twelve months and the decimation of the playing staff, Cobblers secured a 3-2 win with player/manager, Phil Chard scoring a late winner. That proved to be the highlight of the season as for the next eight months, Chard and his battered team had their backs well and truly to the wall.

In the next twenty-four games Chard's tiny squad only managed four wins. Everyone connected with the Club was becoming more and more concerned about the Cobblers' league position. As they slipped further and further down the table, officials and supporters alike became worried as to where the Club was going to finish in Division Three come early May. Wycombe Wanderers were looking odds on favourites to win the Conference. Everyone knew that Wycombe's new Adams Park ground met League standards. If Wycombe won the Conference then a League club would definitely be relegated. Although by then the new community stadium in Northampton was again becoming a distinct possibility, it was some way off. Everyone knew that the County Ground was an embarrassment to both the Club and the League. Certainly ninety-nine per cent of the football world would welcome Adams Park into the fray. Ninety-nine per cent of the football world would not be sorry to see the County Ground fade into the non-league, never to be seen again.

Wrexham Away

In that awful run that saw the Cobblers win only four games in twenty-four, a new Club record was very nearly set . It started on September 15 when Northampton lost 3-0 away at Barnet. In the next six games the team lost every league game they played. This meant that if the side were defeated at Wrexham on October 24 they would set a new and very unwanted Club record. Eight consecutive defeats.

Not only had the days and weeks leading up to the Wrexham game been a nightmare for the Cobblers but they had also been pretty dreadful for me as well. In the week before the game I had taken some annual leave. This was rudely interrupted when I received a hand delivered letter from my employer strongly recommending that I attended a departmental meeting at a nearby hotel on the Wednesday of that week. I at once guessed what it was. Unconfirmed rumours had been spreading that my department was on the verge of being made redundant. On that Wednesday, the manager of the department confirmed my worst fears. He told forty-six of us that we were going to be laid off and our jobs were being outsourced to an external company. Although I had expected this was the reason for the meeting, it still shook me up somewhat to be told that by the start of the new year unemployment could well be a distinct possibility.

The day still had some more surprises in store for me. Firstly the forty-six of us were all offered our old jobs back with the new private company that were taking over our duties. This was not as good as it sounded. Firstly our hourly rate was to be slashed. In fact the figure was so low that it would have put us below the bread line! Also amongst several other nasty little surprises, we would not have been able to claim any sick pay in the first six months of our employment with the new company. I arrived home feeling pretty deflated. That was only the start! Just hours after I had lost my job I was asked for a divorce! Let's just say that I was somewhat surprised at my ex-wife's timing. In the space of four hours I had lost my job, my marriage and with increasing certainty my home.

Three days later I found myself on a bus heading towards North Wales. After a splendid lunch of fish and chips in Nantwich, we pulled up at the Racecourse Ground in Wrexham. The day is still very clear in my mind. In spite of their awful form, Cobblers pulled off a shock 1-0 win with Mickey Bell scoring on the stroke of half-time. Cobblers also played much of the game with only ten men as Ian McPharlane, playing only his second game for Northampton was sent off. Wrexham also managed to squander late chances as goalkeeper Barry Richardson and Steve Terry somehow managed to keep the defence in tact. The away end went mad on hearing the final whistle. As we left Wrexham the double decker bus was a sea of utter joy and contentment. It was as though Cobblers had just lifted the FA Cup. Everybody including myself started singing songs, cheering and clapping. What a game and what a result.

It was probably not until half way home that I suddenly remembered what type of week I had just had. I realised that from the moment I started to eat my fish and chips in Nantwich, I had not thought about redundancy, divorce or losing my house once. Football has a terrible habit of kicking you in the teeth when all seems to be going well, but that day in Wrexham it had certainly come up trumps. My mind had been totally wrapped up in the game and had been reliving the goal over and over again. Looking back now I often wonder how I got through that dreadful week with my marbles still in tact. I now know that the Mickey Bell goal at the Racecourse Ground helped a great deal.

****

On February 27, Northampton lost 3-1 at home to Scarborough. They were now well and truly bottom of the entire league. For all true Northampton supporters it was almost too much to take. I would regularly listen to 606 on Radio 5. Week in, week out, supporters of some of the biggest clubs in the country, if not the world, would come on the line. Their conversation would go along these lines,

"I think that Howard Wilkinson should go. Yes I know Leeds won the league last season but...."

Then one night another caller said,

"Ryan Giggs, what can anyone see in him? Why Ferguson picks him every week I'll never know, and I'm a Manchester United supporter!"

While I'm at home listening to this garbage, my club, Third Division, unfashionable, debt-ridden, smallest squad in the league, three sided ground, in administration Northampton Town have just secured ninety-second spot in the Football League. They are now red hot favourites not to escape the trap door into the Conference. Then you hear some Manchester United supporter on national radio saying that the wonderfully gifted Ryan Giggs is crap. What would a Northampton or Halifax have given for a player of Giggs' stature! Oh and then someone is not happy with their manager Mr Wilkinson who won them the Championship a few months previous! For supporters from Gillingham, Halifax or Northampton success in February 1993 would have been mid-table obscurity in Division Three.

Some supporters of larger clubs just don't know they are born. How can anyone fail to be impressed by Ryan Giggs for crying out loud?! How can anyone ask for Howard Wilkinson's head months after he has lifted the biggest club championship in world football? What would these callers have thought after Warren Hawke, later to secure his fame at Berwick Rangers, had failed to score on a Friday night at York City! Do some of those people phoning 606 really worry that Ryan Giggs is not up to it? If Howard Wilkinson had taken Leeds United to ninety-second in the league, then yes, the caller may have been justified in his argument. But then I don't suppose he has walked down his local chip shop wearing his club colours with pride after getting totally stuffed 8-0 at Lincoln! What possible problems have Manchester United, City or Leeds got or ever have. Until your club is bankrupt or staring relegation from the league in the face, you have no problem.

By the end of March 1993, Northampton Town had only managed eight league wins all season. Then we went to Glanford Park.....

Anyone for Colchester?

It was a Tuesday night. I was sitting at the back of a "Northampton Transport" service bus. It had just made its way on to the M18, a long, long way from home. The time was just past ten o'clock. A hot bath, a nice juicy cup of tea and a warm cosy bed were still around three hours off, if I was lucky! Once the bus had reached its destination at Northampton, I would still have a problem. I did not own a vehicle, how was I going to get another twelve miles to my front door in Olney?

The bus started to eat up the miles of the M18. There were many people on board but there was a deathly hush. The atmosphere was very subdued. I had witnessed this scene before, many times, all over the country. I knew that I would suffer it many times again, but I would still go back for more. That night though, it was the worst I had ever known it. By the time the bus finally made its way down the slipway on to the M1 a few muffled conversations had sprung up. I however, was still silent, deep in my own thoughts. Finally, as Tuesday night became Wednesday morning, a figure made its way very slowly up the bus, clipboard in one hand, pen in the other. He stopped at each row and spoke to everybody making notes on the clipboard.

I had been in Scunthorpe that night. As it was a Tuesday, I had again eaten into my annual leave entitlement. The people I work with cannot understand me. Why do I subject myself to this regularly? I, on the other hand, think they must live very sheltered lives. In spite of the awful events of the evening, I had in some strange perverse way enjoyed myself! It had been a long day. Eight-thirty start at work in the morning. After a bite to eat in the staff canteen I caught the train from Milton Keynes Central to Northampton and then the bus to Scunthorpe in the afternoon. After the events of the evening, it seemed a longer than usual haul home. As I said, it's happened before and it will happen again. As sure as eggs are eggs, whether it is Scunthorpe, Torquay or Burnley. Ah Burnley, that's another story and very similar to this.

We passed Watford Gap service area on the M1. It is always a great feeling when travelling home from the North. Once you pass Watford Gap you know that the next exit is Junction 16 to Northampton. When you have travelled these roads for many years you get to know the landmarks that count down the miles from home. For instance, from the North West, the Walsall turning on the M6 is an hour from Northampton, providing there are no hold ups. Then there is the radio station at Rugby. Nearly home.

The figure finally reached the back of the gloomy bus. Junction 16 was finally upon us. He spoke, his Scots accent breaking through the downcast atmosphere.

"Any bookings for Colchester on Saturday?"

"Yes please", I said, always a glutton for punishment.

"Ten o'clock start."

I must be mad, surely? In spite of the awful night I am pretty certain to be going through the same in a few days time. I just cannot break my habit. Tonight Northampton Town, the team I have supported since I was seven years old, got well and truly stuffed. They had turned up at Scunthorpe along with several hundred supporters, myself as usual included, and had been hammered 5-0! Yes, after following the Cobblers for over twenty years, one does get used to this kind of thing, but that night in Scunthorpe was different. Wycombe Wanderers looked odds on certainties to win the Conference and someone from Division Three looked like they were going out of the League. Unfortunately, it seemed that Northampton were becoming the people's favourites for the drop. After what we had witnessed at Glanford Park that night, it was becoming more and more likely. That was why the bus was so deathly quiet. The Club had survived the recent death penalty from the Court but player/manager Phil Chard and his decimated squad would be lucky to escape from this nightmare.

It was not long into the game when things really started to go wrong for the Cobblers. At half-time they were already 3-0 down. Not only this but they looked poor, very, very poor. It was at this time that an extraordinary thing happened. As the second half kicked off a Cobblers' fan yelled,

"Phil Chard's claret and white army!"

Immediately several others responded,

"Phil Chard's claret and white army!"

The momentum continued and it was not long before just about all the away fans were singing,

"Phil Chard's claret and white army!"

It was an extraordinary scene. There were my beloved Cobblers getting totally stuffed by Scunthorpe and the away fans were cheering their side on like we they were winning the championship. It was strange. John, who had in the past year become a very good friend of mine through work and supporting the Cobblers, actually timed how long the chanting went on for. It was around twenty-two minutes! The Roker roar may be legendary, the Kop unique, but for me this was something quite unprecedented. You had to be there to experience it. The home fans, who had every reason to sing, were totally silent. It was not until their fifth goal hit the back of the net that we heard any vocal encouragement from their end. By that time the long suffering Cobblers' supporters were subdued and the enormity of what was happening had sunk in. The Conference seemed just that bit nearer, that was why the bus was so quiet.

It was almost despair

We were almost resigned to Conference football come August. It was an awful time. Personally, events surrounding the County Ground's survival for another season of League Football started to take over my life. At work, walking down the street, sleeping, in fact all the time, subconsciously I would have the Cobbler's worries on my shoulders.

Football is not the be all and end all of life! Try telling that to three thousand or so regular Northampton Town supporters in 1992/3. The "Will the Cobblers stay up?" burden was there all the time, no matter where you were or what you were doing. It was always at the back of the mind.

April 2 to April 6, a year after the administrator had sacked all those players, saw two of the most important wins in the Club's history. After the nightmare of Scunthorpe, Chard picked the team up and against all the odds secured back to back wins against Rochdale and Bury. A priceless six points and the double over Rochdale. After a goalless draw against Walsall on April 12, Northampton hauled themselves off the bottom of the table. The next two games were away at Colchester and Doncaster (I missed that one). Only one point was picked up after a Cobblers draw at Belle Vue. As many had predicted earlier in the season, Cobblers' league survival was more than likely going to go to the wire. With two weeks of the season left, it was now a three horse race for the drop amongst Halifax, Gillingham and Northampton. Northampton had the most difficult of the three run-ins, high flying Wrexham at home and play-off contenders, Shrewsbury away. Cobblers had not scored at Shrewsbury for thirty years!

April 29 was not a good night. Wrexham only needed to win one of their remaining games to secure promotion. Their fans believed that this was going to be the night. As a result the Spion Kop must have had two thousand highly excited Welsh fans packed in. Added to that, many other people turned up as it was possible that this could be the last league game ever at the County Ground. The attendance given was seven and a half thousand, the biggest league gate Northampton had played in front of all season.

Well before half-time, two goals from Gary Bennett had finished off the contest. Wrexham proved far too strong for Chard's battle-weary players. As the referee blew the final whistle hundreds of Wrexham fans invaded the pitch, jubilant that they had secured promotion. What a contrast to the Hotel End. If Northampton had won they would have been safe. There was now an agonising wait of ten days to know the outcome of the Club's league future.

That Saturday, the other two clubs in the relegation struggle, Gillingham and Halifax, met at the Priestfield stadium. Two second half goals from Gillingham meant their league survival had been secured. What a relief that must have been for them. It was now a two horse race for survival between Halifax and Northampton. Halifax were bottom with thirty-six points, Cobblers then had thirty-eight points. In spite of having fewer points, Halifax were still favourites to stay up. If Northampton won their last game at Shrewsbury they would be safe, no matter what happened at The Shay.

Gay Meadow

8 May 1993. I can still remember the build up to the game and the ninety minutes as if they happened yesterday. However, the week leading up to the game is now a blur. All I really remember is that John and I spent a lot of time that tension wracked week at work discussing what tactics Chard would adopt. We were dreading it. At 16:45 on May 8 we knew Cobblers, our local team, the one we had supported home and away for over twenty years was more than likely to be dropping out of the league. We also knew that the Club had been dealt a cruel blow. Their most influential player, Steve Brown had been harshly dealt with by the referee at Colchester and would be missing due to suspension.

I made my way to Shrewsbury on a Northampton Transport red double decker bus. After mysteriously stopping off for lunch at Telford Shopping Centre (no pubs or fish and chip shops in sight anywhere) the convoy of buses arrived at Gay Meadow, where the Cobblers had never won in my lifetime! There are still disagreements as to how many fans travelled to Shrewsbury that day. My estimate would be around two thousand five hundred. For some fans it was just all too much. The enormity of this game was just too unbearable and many stayed away. I had to go. Whatever happened I had to witness it. I knew that it was more than likely that win, lose or draw, grown men, probably myself included, would be crying at the end of the game. To add to the tension and possibilities, if Shrewsbury won they were in the play-offs. It was all too much to take.

As I disembarked at Gay Meadow I managed to find John who had come up with his mate Clive. Alison, John's wife, had decided to stay away. Forget Fulham in '66 or Crewe in '87, this was now the biggest ever game in the Club's history. We entered the ground. John had brought a radio to hear what was going on at The Shay. As the time ticked away towards kick-off, the tension became more and more unbearable. Anxiety was written on everybody's face. Some fans, in an effort to disguise it, had painted their faces claret and white or wore wigs. Others had brought balloons. By five to three the away end was heaving. The teams came out: D Day for Northampton Town had arrived.

The game kicked off and Gay Meadow was a theatre of noise. The packed away end erupted, balloons and ticker tape were released, the tension of the past season and especially the last ten days came to the surface. Cobblers soon had to soak up a lot of pressure in the early stages as Shrewsbury and especially their centre forward, Carl Griffiths, looked very dangerous. Like John, many of the away supporters had radios or walkmans pressed against their ears, desperate to find out any news from Halifax. It was probably the first and last time that any Northampton fans were willing Hereford to win!

On twenty-four minutes, player/manager Phil Chard conceded a free kick just outside the penalty area. His crude challenge was rewarded with a yellow card. The free kick was taken and the Shrews number three, Lynch, fired the ball past Richardson into the bottom right of the net. As the home fans celebrated there was despair on every face in the away end. Gay Meadow was one of the Cobblers' bogey grounds of all time and it looked like keeping up that tradition. Things then started to hot up. Tackles started to fly in from both sides. Chard then went close to scoring when his free kick was tipped over at full stretch from Paul Edwards. Five minutes later, goalscorer Lynch cleared the ball from deep inside his own half. As it sailed into the Cobblers' half it fell awkwardly for Terry Angus who completely misjudged the bouncing ball. Immediately the dangerous Carl Griffiths, who was proving to be a real handful, pounced. He ran on to the ball, rounded Richardson and fired the ball home past Terry Angus who was desperately trying to get back. Angus, a favourite with the Cobblers' supporters and a player who never gave anything less than one hundred per cent in a claret and white shirt, was distraught. Cobblers held out until half-time without conceding another goal.

As the players headed off towards the changing room, the away end was very subdued. Anyone near a radio craned to hear of an update from The Shay. News came through. Halifax - Hereford was goalless. I suppose it was something, another little thing for the Northampton fans to cling on to. Nobody, but nobody had the remotest idea of what was about to happen.

For the second half, Chard went all out on attack, what else could he do. He pushed himself up front, took the quiet Aldridge off and brought on another attacker, Pat Gavin. In spite of being 2-0 down, the away supporters if anything became more vocal. The encouragement given to the players was almost overwhelming. If the worst happened, and that was looking more and more likely, then the fans were going to give it their all. Almost straight after the sides had kicked off, Kevin Wilkin had a twenty yard effort brilliantly turned over by Shrews goalkeeper Edwards.

It looked like Chard's decision to bring on Gavin was proving to be a wise move. Cobblers had moved up a gear and were starting to look far more threatening. On fifty-one minutes Chard's move paid off. Pat Gavin flicked the ball on towards the Shrewsbury penalty area. As the ball seemed to be going harmlessly towards Edwards, their defender Blake seemed to hesitate. Chard appeared to be chasing a lost cause but he pounced on the error, nipped in past the number five and rounded Edwards firing the ball into the back of the unguarded net. The away fans erupted. Northampton were now well and truly back in the game. There were thirty-nine minutes left.

Cobblers continued to press forward, the crowd almost unable to contain themselves. News from Halifax, as far as we knew, was still 0-0. Cobblers were still in with a shout. Then it happened. Looking at it then and looking back on it now, that was the biggest moment of the afternoon. When it happened I had a sneaking little feeling that this was the turning point. Since that day others I have spoken to also had that feeling. Cobblers were beginning to really fire. Since the half-time substitution they were really looking dangerous. Suddenly the prolific and highly dangerous Carl Griffiths broke free and bore down on goal, one-on-one with Richardson. Griffiths hit the ball from the edge of the area. As Richardson raced out to narrow the angle he was helpless as Griffiths' shot beat him. Incredibly the ball struck a post and failed to cross the line. In the ensuing mayhem the ball eventually ended up in Richardson's hands.

This one moment will probably stick in all Cobblers' fans' memories forever. If one incident throughout the ninety minutes turned the game, then it was this one. If Griffiths had struck that ball one inch further to the left, the stuffing would almost certainly have been knocked out of the Cobblers. The game continued. Northampton still pressed forward. Shots rained in on Paul Edwards' goal from Gavin and Stuart Beavon who was playing his last ever league game before retiring. With eighteen minutes left on the clock the Shrews looked like they might hold out. If Halifax were to score at that moment then Cobblers were a possible eighteen minutes from replacing Wycombe Wanderers in the Conference. It was too much to take. A year before they had survived the winding up axe only for this to happen.

This was the moment that Kevin Wilkin broke down the right-hand side, just managing to keep the ball in play. As he beat the leftback his tame cross was miskicked by Blake and substitute Pat Gavin pounced. He hit the ball on the volley into the roof of the net past a helpless Edwards. 2-2. Over two thousand travelling fans went berserk. Some fans were unable to contain their raw emotion and feelings spilled on to the pitch punching the air. Cobblers had failed to score at Gay Meadow in something like thirty years, now they had scored twice in less than thirty minutes!

In the pandemonium I noticed John's little radio in several pieces on the floor. Incredibly, in spite of the commotion going on around him, he managed to pick it up and put it back together. It still worked! He cannot remember that happening! With the score at 2-2, one of the most incredible moments I have experienced inside a football ground happened. I was standing to the left-hand side of the goal, some way up the terrace. A wave of emotion and startled faces seemed to be spreading from our left. Many people, like John had their ears pressed against radios. Suddenly I realised what was happening. It was confirmed, Hereford had taken the lead at Halifax. Everybody at this point was singing and dancing. I turned around and hugged John. He was crying and he was not the only one. The pendulum was, against all possible odds, starting to swing towards Northampton.

7It was truly incredible. At that moment my head was spinning but my eyes were dry. I was trying to sing along with those around me but nothing would come out of my throat. I was on cloud nine. Whilst this pandemonium was going on, Mickey Bell went perilously close to hitting a third. By now the Cobblers' fans were begging for the final whistle and hoping that Hereford held on for their victory at The Shay. With six minutes left on the clock this action packed thriller of a game was going to have its last twist. Cobblers' goalkeeper Barry Richardson placed the ball down for a goal kick. He pumped the ball up to the half way line where Chard overhit an innocuous pass for Gavin to chase. The ball ran kindly for Blake who passed back to goalkeeper Paul Edwards. Edwards could not of course pick the ball up. In keeping with the spirit in which the Cobblers had played all afternoon, substitute Gavin decided to bear down on Edwards anyway. A lost cause?

Blake had made two errors already that had cost Shrewsbury dearly but this time there was nothing wrong with his backpass. As Edwards met the ball he decided to clear it first time. He connected with the ball as Gavin bore down on him. Astonishingly the ball cannoned off the back of one of Gavin's legs. To the amazement of the entire crowd it ended up nestling in the back of the net. 3-2 to Northampton Town. I had never witnessed and will probably never again witness anything like it. Over two thousand fans went absolutely delirious. Pat Gavin was mobbed by his team mates. Whatever this man achieves in the rest of his life he will be always be regarded as one of the biggest heroes ever to have worn a claret and white top. At this point many Shrews fans left, others were so stunned at what had gone on in the previous thirty nine minutes they just stood motionless on the terraces.

When the final whistle went, the away end emptied on to the playing area. Some supporters just sobbed on the pitch. Others like myself let off nine months of frustration and celebrated in front of the players' tunnel until Phil Chard came out into the stand and acknowledged the hundreds of bewildered fans. Ten days previous, victorious Wrexham had celebrated on the County Ground. Now it was our turn. Nobody and nothing was going to spoil it. It was a miracle that we had survived the Court. It was a fairy tale that we were still a league club.

There was a loser that day. It was not Shrewsbury. They had had a good season only just missing out on a play-off place. The loser was Halifax Town. Our result meant that whatever happened at The Shay was irrelevant. We were not to know that at the time though. For the record Halifax did lose 1-0. Whilst hundreds of Cobblers' fans celebrated at Gay Meadow the opposite happened in Halifax. Hundreds of their fans were also on the pitch but for totally different reasons. They had just ceased to be a league club.

A convoy of buses, mini buses and cars made their way back along the M54 towards Northampton that evening. What celebrations! I had lost John somewhere in the melee on the pitch. That night my mate Fred was in the Olney

41

Town Football Club with me. So pleased was he with the result, that he bought a jug of beer and everyone for once drank to Northampton Town Football Club. In the hours and days after that game, officials, directors and Club President Dave Bowen all said the same thing,

"The Club must never find itself in this position again."

Player/manager Phil Chard had one more task to perform before the Club began its summer break. He had to draw up the retained list. There are always shocks when this list comes out, whoever your team is. This one was no exception. There were two big shocks. Gay Meadow hero Pat Gavin who had just reached cult status was to go, along with one of the most popular figures at the County Ground for years, Terry Angus. Angus was the most surprising decision. A player who always gave his all. Fortunately for those two players they managed to sign for new clubs. Gavin went to Wigan Athletic and Terry Angus joined Fulham. It speaks volumes for these two players that in the months and years to come they were always welcomed back at Northampton with their new clubs. Other players who were once County Ground heroes (Russell Wilcox for instance) would always be greeted with "Cobblers' reject". Gavin and especially Angus never received treatment like this.

When the dust had finally settled after the Shrewsbury game many supporters knew that the battle had only just started. Cobblers had a very small and weak squad. It needed improving. In the back of many people's mind was the nagging feeling that the 1993/4 season was going to be far from easy. The words, *we must never find ourselves in this position again,* could yet come back to haunt the Club.

1993/1994

Rock Bottom.

The aftermath of the Shrewsbury game rumbled on for quite some time. For weeks after the famous victory I found myself being stopped in the street and congratulated by people. The only reason for this was that they knew I was a Cobblers' supporter! Although many locals where I live ridicule the Cobblers, many seemed relieved that the local Football League Club had managed to save their Division Three status. I was on a high for weeks.

On July 26 1993, Northampton Town received the historic news that they had been waiting for many decades! Northampton Borough Council voted by twenty-two votes to fifteen to give final approval for the new community stadium. As it was a community facility the stadium would host local Rugby League, American Football, local cup finals, but most importantly, it would be the new home of Northampton Town Football Club. At that moment it was hoped that the stadium would take twelve months to construct and that the Cobblers would start the 1994/5 season there. For me personally I could not quite believe it. Finally at long last against all the odds, the Cobblers would be moving to a new home. How important that result at Gay Meadow was we will never know. If Halifax had stayed up and Cobblers had gone down then I think it would have been very doubtful whether we would have got a new stadium. Extraordinary when you think that two years before this announcement, Northampton Town had been fighting for its life in the High Court. For me, the day when we played our last ever game at the County Ground could not come quick enough. When the 1993/4 fixture list came out it revealed that the last game at the County Ground would be against Chester City on 30 April 1994.

At the start of the 1993/4 season, most supporters realised that the next nine months were going to be far from easy. The fear was heightened in the lead up to the new season as the Club had a transfer embargo placed on it by the Football League. It appeared that other clubs in the league were not happy that the administrator had extended the administration order for a further twelve months. Although the Cobblers were now trading in the black, they were still paying back creditors and this would last until 1997. The club still owed money to the PFA who had paid some of the Club's wages two seasons previous. Until this was paid in full, Northampton Town could not even sign my Dad on loan. This came as a hammer blow. With all that had gone on since the famous night at The Exeter Rooms in January 1992, this was the last thing on earth the Club wanted. The transfer embargo turned out to have devastating consequences.

It never rains but it pours. The season kicked off on August 14 at Gigg Lane, home of Bury. Due to cricketing commitments I missed this game. If player/manager Chard did not have enough problems before this game, he had when it had finished. He must have wondered if everything was worth it. The result was encouraging, a goalless draw, but one incident was to cloud the entire game. Kevin Wilkin, one of the big heroes from Shrewsbury, was, for many who were present at Gigg Lane that day, looking his sharpest since joining the Club. That was until Lee Anderson took him out with a dreadful foul. It became immediately obvious that Wilkin was in a serious way. Reports after the match confirmed this. The injury was to his knee and it would be another five months before Kevin Wilkin would play again. With the embargo in place, Chard and his assistant John Barnwell could not bring in anyone to replace Wilkin.

From the fence I was sitting on I did not envy Phil Chard one little bit. Managing any league club is stressful enough. Managing one which is strapped for cash with a transfer embargo slapped on it is just about a non-starter. Coupled with all of this, he was supposed to put on a claret and white shirt and try and play football. The next three games after Bury, away at Colchester and Crewe and at home to Walsall, resulted in defeats. The euphoria of Gay Meadow seemed like a lifetime away. Yet again the Club found itself at the wrong end of the table. The talk on the terrace was once again revolving around survival, not progression. On September 18, after managing to pick up a point away at Hereford, Wigan Athletic arrived at the County Ground. In their side was ex-Cobblers hero at Shrewsbury, Pat Gavin. He received a very warm welcome from the Hotel End. There was no "Cobblers' Reject" chant to be heard anywhere. A miserly two thousand two hundred and thirty-five fans turned up and witnessed one of the worst displays of football I have seen on the County Ground by a Northampton side.

Everything was missing from the performance that day. There was no commitment, passion or skill from anyone in claret and white. You could have written the script. Wigan won 2-0. Who else but Pat Gavin scored the first goal. As the ball hit the back of the net many Northampton fans actually cheered! At the end of the game Pat Gavin was cheered off by the Hotel End. Many supporters felt that Chard should not have released Gavin. Although I will never be able to thank Pat Gavin enough for what he achieved at Gay Meadow, in all fairness I think that Chard made the right decision to release him. That argument is backed up when you take into account what he has achieved since he went to Wigan. It would have been sentimental if Chard had kept him on. When he made the decision to release Gavin, Chard had no idea that, come August, the Club would have had a transfer embargo slapped on it. After the game, I stood on the Hotel End, not for the first time in my life, stunned by what I had just seen. A chorus of "What a Load of Rubbish" was ringing in my ears. At that moment, after twenty years or so of following the Cobblers, after all the ups and downs, this felt like the game that tipped the scales. Putting it bluntly, we were crap! There is no other way to describe it. In fact both teams were much of a muchness. There was one bright spot that afternoon though. It was produced by Wigan's number seven, a young lad on loan from Manchester United. His name was Keith Gillespie. Cobblers did not have a clue how to handle him and he was the difference between the two teams. Two years later, Gillespie, now in the United first team squad, signed for high flying Newcastle United in the record breaking Andy Cole transfer. Newcastle got one of the bargains of all time.

It was obvious to all and sundry that the squad of fifteen was just too small and that it was going to be a very, very long winter. As I left the County Ground that evening I wondered just how long Chard would stick it out or alternatively how long before he would be shown the door.

On September 21, news broke that Phil Chard had been sacked as manager of Northampton Town. The Cobblers run of nightmare events seemed to be roller-coasting along as usual. Many fans, including myself, did not quite know how to react to the news. After the events of April 1992 when the administrator had decimated the squad, success for the Cobblers was to avoid finishing bottom of the league come May 1993. Chard had managed this with a way under strength, Conference standard squad. What else was he supposed to do? On the other hand it was rumoured that Chard found it hard to communicate with his players and that his style of management was not liked. On a couple of occasions Chard had publicly criticised the players, one of these being after the Wigan game. It was practically the last thing he performed as manager.

It came as no surprise that Chard's assistant John Barnwell was appointed the new manager of the Cobblers. This appointment seemed to lift not only the players, but many supporters as well. Me included. Barnwell had had a long career in football. His most famous achievement was managing Wolverhampton Wanderers when they won the League cup in 1980. His promotion from assistant to manager of the Cobblers seemed to have an immediate effect. After a battling performance at Lincoln, where Cobblers lost 4-3, Darlington turned up at the County Ground and became the first side to lose against Northampton that season. It had taken until October 2. The next game was against league newcomers Wycombe Wanderers. In front of a crowd of over five thousand, another point was picked up as the two sides battled out an excellent 1-1 draw. These last two results hauled the Club off bottom position. At long last there seemed to be something for the die hard fans to cheer about. Amazingly, ex-manager Phil Chard continued to play for the Club.

On October 12, Mansfield Town were the next team to visit the County Ground. This proved to be the most significant game of the season. It turned Northampton's season on its head. At the end of the game, to the amazement of everyone present, Cobblers had well and truly played Mansfield off the park. Led by an outstanding performance from skipper, Steve Brown, the Stags returned to Nottinghamshire on the wrong end of a 5-1 scoreline. Everything clicked that night. I can remember it so well. The team looked totally unbeatable. It is moments like this that make everything worthwhile. All those treks to the County Ground. All those hauls up and down the country's motorway system. All the hours of torture on freezing cold, windswept terraces. Results like that on October 12 make you just forget everything.

The next morning at work John and I were walking round like Cheshire cats. Still on cloud nine and likely to be so for another twenty-four hours at least, we recounted the match report several times to those who had the fortune, or misfortune, to ask. John, wallowing on the high, recommended that people should nip down the bookies and put money on Cobblers as an outside bet for the play-offs, even though they were still only one place off the bottom of the entire Football League! He was desperately looking forward to the trip north to Scunthorpe that Saturday. Unfortunately I would be moving my sister about three hundred or so miles south of there to Plymouth, thus missing the action. We were confident the Cobblers' season had changed for the better. I was really cheesed off that I would not be at Glanford Park. Mansfield was the turning point, but not in the way we expected.

Four days after beating Mansfield, Cobblers lost 7-0. When I heard the result I again felt guilt. I had not been there to witness it. I had let everyone down. Where were you when Kennedy was shot? Where were you when Thatcher was elected? Where were you when Cobblers lost 7-0 at Scunthorpe? Well when Cobblers lost 7-0 at Scunthorpe I was on the M5 in Somerset. Within a month they were out of the FA Cup, losing yet again to a non-league club, this time with Bromsgrove Rovers doing the damage. Two months after taking charge, John Barnwell's head was wanted on a platter by many Hotel Enders. At the end of the day though his hands were tied like Chard's had been. The Club still had a transfer embargo in place. Barnwell had inherited that squad. During and after the Bromsgrove game some fans were so disappointed at yet another failure by the Club that they threw their claret and whites scarves on to the pitch. Cobblers' goalkeeper Steve Sherwood, who became the oldest player ever to play for the Club, received some rather unpleasant, and in my opinion, unnecessary vulgar criticism during the game. It was becoming more and more important for the Board of Directors to somehow pay off the PFA so that the transfer embargo could be lifted. This was finally achieved in mid-December but engulfed in renewed optimism, the long suffering fans still were not able to witness a Cobblers victory. It would be four months after the Mansfield victory before the Cobblers would win another game. That was an awful long time. It seemed like forever and I was becoming a laughing stock in the office! In an appalling run of form, Northampton failed to win a match in nineteen attempts.

Torquay.

The fifth game in that awful run was away at Torquay. I had ruled out the possibility of going down on the bus. Again, I simply could not afford it. Thankfully, John was going down by car. He had to go into work in the morning and then directly on to Torquay. Would I like a lift down to Plainmoor? Before I could utter the words, "yes please", I had booked a half day off.

On the morning of November 2, I was up at 07:00. I arrived at work early so that I could get as much done as possible before zooming off down to Devon with John. As we sat at lunch in the staff canteen, I'm pretty sure that many of our colleagues thought us completely barmy to be going down to Torquay to see a football game on a Tuesday evening. Others though could understand. It's more than a game of football. It is a way of life.

We were on the road shortly after midday. On this occasion John and I decided to avoid Swindon like a dose of the plague following reports from my sister that she had got stuck in a thirty mile bottleneck there some two days previous. Instead we took the lovely scenic route through Chipping Norton, Stow-on-the-Wold and on to the M5 at Tewkesbury. It was that time of the year when the leaves were turning and were all different colours. As we joined the M5, the claret and white scarf was dangled from the window! It had to be done! We had a toilet stop at Bristol and John phoned Alison. It also gave us a good opportunity to stretch our long legs.

We arrived in Torquay with plenty of time to spare at 17:00. After such a long journey we were in need of some nourishment and liquid refreshment. John parked up near the ground. We decided that we would have a pint or two before eating. We headed down towards the sea front. Could we find a pub? Like hell could we! Eventually we came across one. It was called "The Manor". By now we had been walking for quite some time. It had also started to rain and we were soaking! We went straight in. If it had not been for the fact that we had been hunting for so long, we would have walked straight back out again. It took ages for us to get served. The beer was passable but we could hardly hear ourselves talk above the din of the music channel that was playing on the television screens. There were also many locals who seemed to have been in there most of the day. To put it mildly they seemed rather intoxicated. Not the best place I have been in. We decided not to stay. Finding another establishment proved to be difficult but we succeeded. By now we were some way from the ground. The pub was called "Chaplins" and was completely the opposite of "The Manor". Inside was very pleasant and it served a good pint. Being so early in the evening it was very quiet. There were only four other men drinking at the bar. When John went off to the gents I could not help but overhear some of their conversation. One of them was openly discussing his forthcoming sex change with the others!

Time was getting on. We found a local chip shop/cafe type affair and decided to eat tea there. As John had driven down and paid for the petrol I insisted on paying for the food. The diner we had found was quite astonishing. Although the place was empty and we were the only ones eating there, it took the assistant five minutes to calculate John's chicken and chips, and whatever I was eating. Eventually he rang up this figure on the till. To this day I'm convinced he still calculated it wrong. What on earth it would have been like in there if it had been busy I hate to think! I have never stayed in Torquay in the summer. I only hope that the facilities and service are somewhat better than they are out of season.

After wining and dining we wandered back up towards Plainmoor and arrived there twenty minutes before kick-off. We asked a steward where the away end was situated and promptly ended up in the home end! John said that the ground was much improved. (This was my first time to Plainmoor.) The floodlights though seemed very dim and left a lot to be desired. The game kicked off. As I looked around me I noticed that the game was entirely policed by the Club's stewards. There were no police about anywhere. It was a good job really. Sitting in front of us was a character who, if the police had been within earshot, would not have lasted two minutes before being either ejected or arrested for foul and abusive language. He was not violent and was no threat to anyone, except the linesman! Most people, including John and myself, were in stitches listening to him. Right from the first minute he started to heckle the linesman. His tirade lasted the whole of the game.

"Oi, linesman you ****, yes you, you ****ing ****. That was never offside. Why don't you stick that ******* flag up your **** you ****!"

You many think that I have exaggerated here. I have not. There was a stand full of witnesses. Every time the linesman ran past the stand he would start up,

"Oi lino, you ****!"

On the very few occasions the linesman ran past without getting abused, other people in the stand yelled out for him,

"Oi linesman you ****!"

At one point in the first half he was abusing the linesman so much with vulgar criticisms that a steward decided to intervene. The steward was very good. There was no heavy-handed approach. Just a word. Our friend was very apologetic. He assured the steward that his foul tirade would stop immediately. The steward left the stand. Immediately the linesman ran down the touch line.

"Oi linesman you ****!"

Again we were all in stitches. For the only time I can ever remember at a football league game, the linesman actually stopped looking at the match and turned round and stared at our "friend" in the stand. The game was still going on. What entertainment!

Cobblers held out until the eighty-first minute before player/manager Don O'Riordan put Torquay ahead. The fact that Torquay had taken the lead made me feel sick but the player who scored it made me feel even worse. Many Cobblers' fans, including myself remember Don O'Riordan from his Notts County days. In a game against the Nottingham club at the County Ground, O'Riordan was attacking well into the Cobblers' half. As he made his way into the penalty area O'Riordan seemed to overrun the ball and it started to head out for a goal kick. This was the moment when he appeared to be shot by a sniper somewhere in Abington Avenue. He fell very dramatically, like a sack of potatoes. The Hotel

End erupted with anger at this piece of kidology only for the referee to blow his whistle and point to the penalty spot. Needless to say the penalty was converted past Peter Gleasure and Notts County went on to win the game!

Just before the final whistle, with Cobblers desperately pushing for the equaliser, Torquay hit a second. A cruel blow for all of us who had travelled the long distance down to Devon on that Tuesday night. In spite of the result though, I had really enjoyed myself. Now for the long haul home. We got to Exeter and pulled off the motorway. After a very swift pint of Bass we were back on the road. Thank goodness we don't support Darlo or Exeter. These type of journeys happen every other week!

By Bristol John was really starting to flag. We opted for the sensible approach and pulled off at the services. We had a pot of tea and some fresh air before hitting the road again. We stopped again between Swindon and Oxford for another break, both of us knackered. Finally John dropped me off in Olney at 02:30. By this time we had both got a second wind and were wide awake! As usual I was glad to get home. I put on the kettle, had a cup of tea and clambered into bed for 03:00. Sleep took some time in arriving, my mind still full of our evening out in Torquay. I was rudely awakened at 07:00. The alarm was shrilling. Somehow I clambered out of bed, I don't know how I managed it but I did. I sorted the cat out and caught my lift to work. I felt dreadful. Totally shattered. This must have been the closest I had ever come to being jet lagged. John had taken the morning off work. I was not so lucky. I was booked on a course for 09:00 that morning. I just had to go in. Fortunately as the morning progressed I felt more and more human.

My day out to Torquay had lasted around twenty-one hours. I must have squeezed in about three hours sleep before going back to work. After days like that, I have often asked myself, was that worth it? Even after a 5-0 defeat on a Tuesday night in Burnley or a 2-0 defeat at Torquay, the answer is always yes.

Even with the Club now strengthening its squad with signings, it was not until February 5 at Carlisle that they managed the all important victory. By winning that game, Cobblers failed to set a new club record number of games without a win, thank goodness, but it had left them marooned at the bottom of the Football League. As you have probably gathered I miss very few games. Typically, the win at Brunton Park was one of them. I simply could not afford to go. My mortgage was taking most of my money. What remained went mostly to my solicitor to pay for the divorce that my ex-wife had insisted upon. I would have loved to have been there. When the result came through on Grandstand I celebrated in my little terraced house with a cup of tea. (Yes, times were that hard!) I would loved to have been on that bus coming home. I bet the atmosphere was one of sheer relief and joy. In spite of the win, Cobblers were still well and truly stuck at the bottom. This time though most supporters thought it inevitable that the Club would finish ninety-second in the league. It was utterly and totally demoralising. The only real bright spot of that season was the fact that Kidderminster were running away with the Conference. This may sound mercenary but it assured that whoever finished bottom of Division Three would not be relegated. Kidderminster's ground was not up to League standard and the Club had failed to meet the December 31 deadline for improvements. For the remainder of the 1993/4 season and beyond, there was a big outcry and support for Kidderminster. David Mellor, the host of the Radio 5 Live programme 606 was a big part of this. Thankfully for clubs like the Cobblers who were struggling at or near the bottom of the Football League, barring a hideous string of results from Kidderminster this meant that they were safe from dropping into the non-league.

As Cobblers' number of games without a win increased towards February, the fans were once again haunted by the fact that they were struggling to avoid finishing last. For the second year running, my whole life seemed to focus around one thought and one thought only, Cobblers' continued and prolonged struggle. I know it's sad, but it's true. Personally I received a great deal of mickey-taking and constant wind-ups about the Cobblers. After twenty or so years of supporting them I was used to it! Nothing was going to change me. I simply could not throw my claret and white allegiance away and support another club. Northampton Town is part of me. It is a way of life just like any other club is to any other loyal supporter. If anything Cobblers' long struggle against bankruptcy and now relegation, only made me more loyal towards the cause.

After the fantastic win at Carlisle, the Cobblers' season picked up somewhat. Their next away match also turned into three points as Walsall were defeated 3-1 at The Bescott Stadium. In spite of the upturn in fortune, Cobblers still remained rooted to the bottom of Division Three where they had been since early November. Barnwell had made some interesting signings after the transfer embargo had been lifted in December. One of these was a Cameroon Under-21 international called Efon Elad. In his first few games he really looked the business. To make him feel at home I managed to get hold of a Cameroon national flag which I daubed with NTFC. For the rest of the season I took it to all the away games! Sad, I know. After the Walsall win though, he seemed to struggle with fitness and never seemed to regain his initial sharpness. It was one up for me at work though. Nobody believed me when I told them that Cobblers had signed an international! The other interesting signing for me was Ray Warburton. Barnwell signed him on loan from York City on the eve of the Carlisle game. Barnwell had not covered himself in glory since his appointment to the hot seat. He had equalled the most awful record ever by a Northampton manager of nineteen games without a win. This though for me was the best move he ever made as manager of the Cobblers. Warburton was the former captain of York but was struggling to get back into their side after suffering a serious leg injury and glandular fever. After seeing just one game from him I was astonished that York had let him go on loan. For me, the reason Northampton's form picked up that season and that they were staying within touch of the rest of the Division was down to Warburton. He was and is a class player. It was refreshing to see that quality of player actually turning out in claret and white. Warburton was also on the receiving end of the worst challenge I have ever witnessed on a football field. That includes all standards of football I have watched. It took place in the terrific 3-1 win at Walsall. As he headed a clearance away, Walsall's number five, Kiester, jumped late, elbow first straight at Warburton's throat. As Kiester connected, Warburton went down like a sack of spuds. It was sickening. You can nearly always tell when a player is badly hurt. If the injury is serious such as a broken limb or a torn ligament the player concerned hardly moves. Warburton was very still on the ground. Initially I thought Kiester had killed him. Physio, Dennis Casey was straight on and thankfully, after some considerable time, Warburton struggled to his feet. He managed to complete the game. The referee had no choice but to send Kiester off.

No sooner had Cobblers' form picked up and somehow hauled them off the foot of table than once again their form slumped. In three consecutive home games in April, Gillingham, Rochdale and Torquay, Cobblers succeeded in losing. Amongst these was defeat at Shrewsbury (no repeat performance this time) and an admirable 1-1 draw at Preston. At Deepdale, Cobblers were leading 1-0 after a Darren Harmon goal until the final minute when Ainsworth fired past Richardson. Thankfully for Cobblers, Kidderminster were still top of the Conference and the new Sixfields Stadium was well under way. They were still in deep trouble but life had to go on.

Christopher Martin.

30 April 1994 was billed as one of the biggest days ever in Northampton Town Football Club's history. Chester City were the visitors that day. It was a huge game for no other reason than it was to be the last ever played at the County Ground, Abington Avenue.

Perhaps the most emotional part of the entire afternoon came before kick-off when the Club chaplain, Reverend Peter Naylor, led a service on the pitch. The reason for the service was to remember Christopher Martin, a supporter and ball boy of the Cobblers who tragically died on 25 February 1970 after a long and courageous battle against Hodgkin's Disease. One of the wishes that Christopher Martin had expressed before he passed away was for his ashes to be scattered on the County Ground. Back in 1970 the Club carried out his wish. Before the game against Chester City, the Cobblers had received a request from his family in Grimsby to see if it was possible to commemorate this occasion before the Club moved to their new home at Sixfields. With the assistance of Reverend Naylor, the Bishop of Brixworth, the parents of Christopher Martin and club director Brian Lomax, a small service was carried out on the pitch. It was a tremendous credit to both sets of supporters present that, throughout the service, you could have heard a pin drop. Although I and many of the people around me were not churchgoers, there were a number of individuals with moist eyes when it had finished. Mr and Mrs Martin must have felt very proud of their son at that moment. Be it even for a very short period of time, he had moved the lives of a great many people from both Northampton and Chester.

The game kicked off in dramatic fashion. With only seconds gone, Warburton intercepted well into the Cobblers' half. He fed Elad who passed on to Kevin Wilkin who fired home a terrific shot from the edge of the area. Most of the crowd went mad as Wilkin was mobbed. There were just eighteen seconds gone on the clock. Try writing a script like that! Well that was about that really. High flying Chester huffed and puffed, Cobblers held on and secured three precious points. Because of the historic nature of the game a larger than usual attendance was present that day (nearly six and a half thousand). When the final whistle was blown, football at the County Ground came to an end. Hundreds of fans raced on to the pitch. The players though did not come out to greet them. The atmosphere had been subdued considerably by news that Darlington, one place below Cobblers at the foot of the League had won 3-0 in a shock result at Mansfield. Barnwell and his team had a big job to do the next week away at Chesterfield. For the second year running, the Cobblers' last game of the season would decide whether or not they would finish bottom. After the initial rush on to the pitch, Fred and I took our handicapped friend George on to the hallowed County Ground pitch. All three of us wanted to soak up the atmosphere of the place before it vanished forever. One thing was certain though after the Chester win. Barring a freak mathematical set of results, Kidderminster would be crowned as Conference champions. The League had again confirmed that nobody would be relegated.

Chesterfield.

From every angle this game was a total and utter nightmare. I had gone up to Chesterfield with John and Alison. We arrived with plenty of time to spare and made our way to a pub about two hundred yards from the ground. Both Cobblers and Chesterfield supporters mixed together with no problems. Not an unusual sight. After a couple of pints we walked to the ground. There seemed to be many police on duty outside the ground. In the eighties there were a number of serious incidents between so-called Northampton and Chesterfield fans. In one of these incidents a policewoman ended up with serious head injuries. It was no surprise to see the police presence. We entered the ground. The away end was packed. The inside of the stadium was totally policed by stewards. Considering the importance of the game and past incidents many of us were surprised to see none of the local constabulary present.

From the moment the game kicked off there seemed only one team in it. There was to be no repeat of Gay Meadow twelve months previous. Cobblers looked very lack lustre. Chesterfield looked the hungrier of the two sides and by half-time they had a two goal lead. Then one of the worst moments of following the Cobblers in twenty odd years happened. It was so unnecessary. During periods of the first half it was evident to all and sundry that some people in the visitors section of the stand to our left were not really there for the football. These so-called fans kept running down a stairway that led to the pitch and were positioning themselves very close to it. The stewards responded not by calling in the police just in case, but by blocking off the stairway with a lady steward who, from where I was standing, seemed barely five foot tall and very petite. I do not wish to sound sexist but it was totally ineffectual and very unfair on her. The atmosphere was obviously tense and you could almost tell what was going to happen. Whoever was in charge of the ground security of this game was making an enormous mistake.

When the players had trooped off the pitch, as if on cue, the inevitable happened. The tiny steward was brushed to one side as half the away section of the stand emptied on to the pitch. For the next five minutes or so all hell broke out on the pitch. The stewards seemed powerless to do anything. Where were all the police who had been so evident outside the ground before the game now? It is hard to say how many individuals actually invaded the pitch. I would estimate around a hundred. For the genuine supporter these scenes were mind blowing. Week in, week out, month in, month out, there are never problems like this. Northampton Town is not a name associated with violence. Every once in a blue moon though, they turn up somewhere. As most genuine supporters of all clubs are aware, violence in the fashion we were seeing at Chesterfield is very rare. Who were these people damaging the good name of Northampton Town like this? There were very few on the pitch whom I recognised.

The trouble on the pitch was becoming more widespread. More and more incidents seemed to be sparking up. Still there were no police present. After what seemed a lifetime the police arrived on the scene. The damage though had been done. The name of football had been dragged through the mud again. The police herded most of the troublemakers back into the stand. A vast majority of the supporters who had remained on the terrace, including myself, jeered and booed at them. Tempers amongst a great many of loyal supporters were pushed to the limit. Northampton Town is a part of life. Over the seasons the supporters have built up a good reputation. It speaks volumes that many of us have mixed with supporters from other clubs before games. Before the Chesterfield debacle I personally had mixed and drunk with other fans at Wigan, Hereford and Walsall to name but a few, never with a hint of bother. This reputation was now going up in smoke.

By the time everyone had been removed from the pitch, the police asked John Barnwell to come out from the changing rooms and appeal for calm. He did so. As he was escorted back to the changing room the element that had invaded the pitch cheered him from the stand. It was totally humiliating. The sad thing was that many who had caused this trouble seemed proud of their achievements. I wonder if they were proud when a man was wheeled round the pitch in front of us on a stretcher with his head split open? For the only time in my life I felt ashamed to be connected with Northampton Town Football Club.

The second half commenced. To be honest I was so angry that a lot of the detail is a blur. Early on in the second half, Cobblers conceded a third goal in bizarre fashion when a shot bobbled hideously in front of Richardson and ended up in the back of the net. When the final whistle came Chesterfield had won 4-0. The Cobblers' performance seemed to lack commitment from certain quarters. We stood on the terrace straining our ears to hear news of how Darlington had got on. Rumours had cruelly been spread that they had in fact lost. It was not until we were back at John's car that the full horror of the afternoon rounded itself up in wonderous style. Darlington had won 1-0 at home to Bury. That result had hauled them off the bottom of Division Three and placed Northampton Town at the bottom for the first time ever in their history. The only glimmer of any type was that Kidderminster had been confirmed as champions of the Conference. For their supporters there must have been frustration that day and our name must have been mud.

It had been an appalling day all round. As we travelled back down the M1, John, Alison and I were very, very subdued. We were deep in our own thoughts. Football sometimes feels like it is the be all and end all of life. I felt completely deflated. The whole season had been an uphill struggle crowned off with humiliation at Saltergate. Many fans, including myself, found ourselves apologising to the Chesterfield stewards on our way out. The policing of the game though had left a lot to be desired. I am certainly not trying to defend that actions of anyone who went on the pitch. They were a total and utter disgrace. However, it was apparent very early on that there was a nasty atmosphere in the ground and especially the away stand. Coupled with the problems that the two clubs had experienced in the 1980s, it did not need a genius to realise that although it very seldom happens, there was likely to be trouble that afternoon. It is all well and good saying after the event, this should have happened or that should have happened but the decision by whoever was in charge not to have a police presence in the ground was a mistake.

As we continued our journey home that evening the wave of sympathy for Kidderminster continued on the 606 programme. It was certainly cruel luck on them. At the end of the day though, the League had a December 31 deadline whereby all Conference grounds had to meet League standard. Kidderminster's ground did not reach that standard by the deadline given. However cruel or unfair they may have thought it was, they knew the rules.

Personally I found and still find the ruling on relegation from the Football League puzzling. With Northampton Town, the club I have supported all my life, finishing bottom in 1994, what I am about to say may seem rather biased. Let me just state the following. I have no problem with clubs from the Conference coming into the Football League. It is the manner in which it happens that bothers me. If Northampton had been relegated in May 1994 then yes, of course I would have been upset. It would have been tragic for the Club and the town if the Cobblers had ended up in the Conference. Saying that though, my loyalty would not have wavered. If come the 1994/5 season I had had to travel to Gateshead on a Tuesday night, then yes I would have been there.

Since automatic relegation from the Football League was introduced, there has been only one real success story. Barnet fans may feel miffed as to why I have not included them as a success story from the Conference but I will come on to that in a while. When Halifax were relegated in May 1993, Wycombe Wanderers were promoted to the Football League. Although it is absolutely no consolation for anyone at The Shay, Wycombe deserved their promotion to the League. They were a forward thinking club. Their Adams Park ground was better than many grounds in Division Three. It certainly shamed the County Ground. Wycombe had a strong squad with, in my opinion, one of the best managers outside the Premier League. Although I am not privy to such information, financially they seemed to be healthy. That, above all other things, is critical to long term survival in the Football League. Many clubs in the Football League have battled against crippling financial debts, Northampton, Aldershot, Bristol City, Brighton and Wolves to mention but a few. It's a big leap up into the Football League. Squads need to be increased with full time wages. Grounds need to be able to cope with large away followings. Before you say, "what on earth is he on about?", remember what happened to Scarborough on their first ever day in Division Four. In their wisdom the League fixture list had Scarborough's opening league fixture at home to the mighty Wolves. Even in the bottom division of the Football League, Wolves were a huge club and they still had a massive following. Unfortunately Scarborough's little Seamer Road ground was the scene of crowd trouble as a massive army of Wolves fans ended up on the North East coast. Who knows what financial and psychological damage scarred Scarborough that day? Clubs who come up from the Conference must have finances and facilities in place to be ready for this type of thing.

Even Wycombe were somewhat taken a back when the Cobblers turned up at Adams Park on 22 January 1994. In spite of being seven points adrift at the bottom of Division Three, Northampton took a massive number of supporters to the Buckinghamshire club. As kick-off fast approached, the away terrace given to us was starting to heave with people. Many fans were still queuing outside. Wycombe sensibly decided to move some of their home fans out of the terrace behind one of the goals and open it up for away support. It was nice to see some common sense, but they were obviously surprised that a club such as Northampton Town could in fact bring one and a half to two thousand fans away from home. I do not want to sound like I am pooh poohing Conference and non-league clubs here but the Football League is a totally different kettle of fish. Of the non-league clubs that have been promoted to the League (not including Darlington and Colchester), Maidstone have gone bust, Barnet were a stone's throw away from the same and Scarborough suffer some of the lowest crowds in the entire League.

What is the solution to the farcical situation that arose at the end of the 1993/4 season? (And 1994/5 and 1995/6?) Personally I think that it could be made pretty simple. In spite of my Club holding on to its League status by a hair's breadth, I still think that there should be some method by which non-league clubs can get into the Football League. Personally I think that the old system of seeking re-election should be re-introduced for the side that finishes bottom of the League. There should be a format by which the voting should take place. What is the state of the club who is finishing bottom of the league? Is their ground up to standard? Do they have an annual struggle against re-election? Are their finances in a healthy state? Then the club finishing top of the Conference should meet some standards. What is the state of their ground? Are they financially stable and are their attendances big enough to finance a Football League outfit?

If, for arguments sake, at the end of the 1992/3 season this format had been in place then I'm sure that Wycombe Wanderers would still have been elected to Division Three. They were a club in the Conference with a football league set up throughout. Halifax though, I'm pretty sure would not have received much sympathy. They were annual strugglers. They were suffering continual financial problems and barely got crowds of more than one thousand five hundred. At the end of the 1993/4 season, this system could have been a very close run thing. Kidderminster's system was not as slick as that of Wycombe. Their ground was declared not up to league standard. Would Kidderminster have been able to have survived in the Football League or would they have gone the same way as Maidstone United? We may never know. There was also talk at the time when they were running away with the Conference that Kidderminster were talking of ground sharing with West Bromwich. This may have only been short term but in my opinion ground sharing is a one way trip to a severe headache. For Maidstone United it proved to be more than a headache. As you know, Northampton finished bottom of the Division in 1993/4. Northampton had suffered bad financial problems. They had recently been under an administration order. However, when they finished bottom that season, the Club's accounts were in the black. Although Northampton's County Ground was one of the worse grounds in the Football League, they were due to move into a brand new all-seater stadium at the start of the next season. This could only be beneficial to the Third Division.

As it was, Northampton Town survived for another year of league football. Kidderminster must have felt pretty sick. I say again, if Northampton had been relegated I would still have been following them all over the country. That would and never will alter. I will not deny that I was relieved that we were still a League Club. I'm sure most Kidderminster fans will not thank me for that.

As John, Alison and I pulled off the M1 at junction 16 after the Chesterfield humiliation, I felt it was the end of an era. That day was the lowest of the low. Things could only get better? The County Ground was now a memory. Sixfields was on the way. New seasons always bring renewed hope. Some believed that the County Ground suffered from a Saturday jinx! Northampton's home record on Saturdays had been appalling. They really did seem to struggle. If you look at the last few seasons there, records will actually support this theory! My reckoning is that whatever atmosphere and noise was created at the County Ground was lost over the cricket pitch or over where the main stand used to be. Nothing seemed to keep any noise in the ground there. 7 May 1994 was the end of an era and I for one was grateful, in more ways than one.

The new era started on 8 May 1994. On this day I asked a girl out who worked in the department next to mine. Since my marriage had ended nearly two years previous, I had neither the financial resources nor the inclination to consider such things. Times change though. From this day on, both mine and the Cobblers' fortunes took a turn for the better.

1994/1995

A New Era.

The nasty sting left in the tail of the 1993/4 season had one more little surprise in store for the fans of Northampton Town. Well before a ball had been kicked in anger for the new season, it was announced that the Club would have to play their first four home league games of the season not at the new Sixfields Stadium but at the old ramshackled County Ground. Although from the outside Sixfields looked all but ready, there was still a great deal of work that had not been finished in time for the new season. So Chester City were not to be the last club ever to visit the County Ground. This honour was to fall to Mansfield Town on 4 October 1994. Before I said good-bye to the County Ground again, it was going to have one more laugh at me. Of the four league games and one Coca Cola cup tie played there at the start of the season, Northampton managed only one win! That came against Carlisle who went on to walk the title. I was on holiday at the time and missed the game, so I never did see another victory there after the Chester game!

The County Ground had for twenty-two years become part of my life but on 4 October 1994, it had stopped being so. It was an end of an era, not just for me, not just for all the Cobblers' supporters from many generations, but for the football world in general.

With us for the grand finale against Mansfield was Peter from Edinburgh who had just started working for the same company as me. It was his first and only visit there. I had been introduced to Pete on his first day when he had joined our little lunchclub for dinner. Straightaway, as usual, the conversation turned to football. As it was a Monday, analysis of the Cobblers, Villa, Derby and Leicester games cropped up. It then emerged that Peter has Heart of Midlothian running through his veins. Talk soon went on to the year when Hearts were odds on to win the Scottish Premier League. Going into the last game Hearts, unbeaten in ages, only had to win against Dundee to secure the championship. Even if they lost, Celtic then had to win by a large scoreline to stand a hope. Tragically Hearts lost and Celtic managed to secure the title. Hearts fans could not believe it. Most people will remember the television pictures of the Jambo fans weeping on the terraces. Peter was one of them. When he told us about this I swear his eyes became moist. The memory still hurt a great deal. It just goes to show what football can mean to some supporters. How many of us still become choked when we watch the Cobblers/Shrewsbury video?

We left for the Mansfield game early as a large crowd was expected. I warned Peter that the County Ground was probably the worst ground in the league since Halifax had been relegated. His true colours then came out when he said that the County Ground could not be as bad as Hibs! As I have only ever been to Forfar, Motherwell (for two night games) and Falkirk north of the border, I'll have to trust him on that one. I had been dreading the Mansfield game. However much the County Ground had been part of my life, I had had enough of it. Its disfigurement, its three sides, its rubbish results, the smelly, inhuman, vile lavs and the burger stands. I had also seen Sixfields close up and knew that it was so near but so far.

Arriving in the Hotel End John and Alison joined us. Alison had just been interviewed by BBC East. The next morning we found out that her interview had gone national on BBC1, Radio 5, Radio 4 and local radio! The game started and Mansfield had obviously won the toss and decided to change ends so that Cobblers had to kick into the Kop for the second half. You then just get the feeling that things are not going to go your way. Ten minutes later this fear was confirmed when Gareth Williams put an easy chance wide from eight yards that looked easier to score than anything I'd seen since an Aldershot player had rounded Peter Gleasure and promptly missed an open goal. Within minutes Wilkinson had scored for Mansfield with a tame shot that went in off the post. Cobblers tried the long ball game against a good looking defence and Aldridge's pace was brought on far too late. On occasions Mansfield looked dangerous coming forward and on the night they never looked in trouble.

The final whistle came. That was it, no more County Ground. I was relieved and felt no emotion. I didn't know whether to be saddened or not by this but it was the end of an era and Sixfields could not come quick enough. I did not want to go on the pitch this time. I had done that after the Chester game. I had said my good-byes that day with all my friends around me. I did not hang around but left the County Ground for the last time. I shed no tears, I was just relieved.

The scramble to get tickets for the opening game at Sixfields against Barnet was almost unprecedented. Fortunately Fred and I were lucky but George and my girlfriend Sharron missed out. Such was the interest in the game that you probably could have filled Sixfields again, demand was that great. I was like a child that Saturday morning I was so excited. Soon after lunch Fred and I set off towards Northampton, we gave ourselves plenty of time to get there! It was an unusual feeling as we approached the Barnes Meadow roundabout on the edge of town. Instead of

The County Ground boiler room being demolished

61

taking the right-hand lane to the Bedford Road we headed left towards St James and on to Duston where we joined the throng of people and vehicles heading towards our new ground. Eventually Fred parked up near the new McDonald's and we wandered towards the ground. As we looked down from the hill towards the stadium, it was hard not to be choked. Two and a half years earlier, the Club was days, if not hours, from being wound up and they were playing at a tip. Now we looked down on the newest stadium in the Football League. In the space of four days Northampton Town had gone from having the worst ground in the league to having a fantastic new all-seater community stadium. Words in this book can never express how proud I felt on that day.

I entered Sixfields for the first time. Although kick-off was still an hour away the place was filling fast. It was a sea of colour. The claret seats, the amber and black of the Barnet, the bright green pitch and dozens of different coloured balloons everywhere. As three o'clock approached, there were still long queues trying to get into the ground. It was no surprise that an announcement was made that the kick-off would be delayed by fifteen minutes due to congestion. Finally the teams came out, Cobblers led by their skipper Ray Warburton. There were a number of people, grown adults who at this point struggled to keep their eyes dry! Personally I was not too bad. Looking back on it, I reckon I was too stunned to get emotional. The entire afternoon seemed to be like a dream. Were the events rolling out in front of me really happening? Was this really the new home of the Cobblers?

The game itself was a cracker. Both sides were obviously lifted by the terrific surroundings, the full gate and the emotion of the occasion. The first half passed in a flash, both goalkeepers earning their corn with terrific saves. Cobblers came closest to opening the scoring when Gareth Williams hit the bar from long range with Barnet goalkeeper Gary Phillips struggling. It was end to end stuff. The second half continued where the first had left off. Who was going to be the first player to score at Sixfields? The North Stand, which had now become the adopted Hotel End, was doing its best to suck the ball into the Barnet net.

Then it happened. A high ball was pumped up field by Darren Harmon. It was controlled by Martin Aldridge who turned the defender. He shot over Gary Phillips who managed to get a hand to the ball but could not stop it nestling in the back of the net. Six and a half thousand people erupted. What a moment. History had happened and would be remembered forever in the life of the Cobblers. Aldridge somersaulted in front of the North Stand. Many people had already burst out crying! Football can be a cruel game. By now Cobblers were dominating affairs. In spite of this, seven minutes after their goal, Dougie Freedman, one of the most prolific strikers in the lower Divisions at that time, equalised for Barnet. Now, just under a thousand Barnet fans were going mad! Cobblers though continued to press forward. In an incredible period of pressure Barnet managed to hold out as Cobblers hit the woodwork a further three times. How on earth Gareth Williams did not score that afternoon I will never know!

When the final whistle went there seemed great disappointment amongst the home supporters. It would have been nice to win our first ever match at Sixfields but at least Barnet did not catch us on the break and really rub our noses in it

Darren Harmon moments before kick off against Barnet

Fred and I strolled out of the ground and headed towards the car. Looking back at the new stadium I was filled with an enormous sense of pride. The County Ground was history. This was our future now. However, in spite of the rose tinted spectacles of Sixfields, the season had a long way to go. Cobblers really needed to be lifted by it all and to put a good string of results together to pull away from the bottom of the Division. Fred and I arrived back at his car. The car park was so full that we knew we were going nowhere for at least half an hour. As we sat there listening to the football results, the whole afternoon was brought into perspective. Over the road to our left somebody had collapsed. Immediately there were St John's Ambulance and police on the scene. From what I could see things were looking serious. Whoever it was was fighting for their life. It was some time before they were put into the ambulance and with the police trying to clear some of the traffic out of the way, rushed off to hospital. By the Monday it had been confirmed that a man had collapsed. Tragically he had died. Although it will not be a crumb of comfort to that man's family, there was one thought in my head when I read the newspaper the following Monday. For him personally, he had probably seen one of his big dreams happen. He had seen his club play at a brand new stadium which none of us had thought would ever happen. It had been a fantastic afternoon. The game had been excellent with an atmosphere to match. He must have been very content just before he passed away.

Four days after the Barnet game John and I travelled to Cambridge to watch the Cobblers play at the Abbey Stadium in an Auto Windscreens Shield group match! Barnwell had put several of the reserves in the team including reserve goalkeeper Mark Ovendale. I feel there is something special about the goalkeeping position. Perhaps it was because I used to play in that position in my Olney Town Sunday Reserve days! Or perhaps it is something to do with goalkeepers having a close affiliation with spectators as they spend nearly all of their time in close proximity to them? Anyway, Ovendale was another goalkeeper to put with the names Gleasure, Starling, Jayes, Parton, Beresford and Hitchcock. There is something romantic about these Auto Windscreen games. I reckon it is because people think that they are a waste of time and that you must be mad to go to them. I would strongly disagree. For John and me, that night in Cambridge has gone down in history as a truly brilliant night out. There were several reasons for this:

i) Cobblers won 3-1.

ii) Neil Grayson scored probably the best goal I have ever seen from a player in claret and white. As their goalkeeper Filon cleared a backpass, it went straight to Grayson. He looked up, took a couple of steps forward and lobbed him from about forty-five yards. His first ever goal for Northampton.

iii) Many Cobblers' fans spent a lot of time singing the following to the home fans:

"Shit ground no fans, shit ground no fans!"

For once they were totally justified.

The Sixfields honeymoon was to last just one more game. Grayson followed up his Cambridge debut goal with another in the very next game at home to Wigan when Cobblers scraped a 1-0 victory. Initially, the atmosphere of moving to a new stadium seemed to lift Barnwell's players but in the next seven games Cobblers managed only two league points and were dumped out of both the FA Cup at Peterborough (4-0) and the Auto Windscreen Shield in a dreadful performance at home to Swansea City (1-0). Probably the 4-0 defeat at London Road was the worst place on earth it could have happened. By now many fans were screaming for the head of Barnwell. Others though were not ready for him to be dumped. Vocal criticism of him was getting more widespread and noticeable with every game. Everybody is entitled to their opinion but what I found disappointing was that most of the criticism aimed at Barnwell occurred whilst the games were taking place. The squad had little confidence left and this did not help. By early December my opinion of Barnwell was beginning to change. Football managers are only human and cannot perform out on the pitch, that is down to his players. Managers though do decide who plays, what tactics are used and what system is to be played. It is also down to him to instil as much confidence and self belief into his players as possible. It is easy for the likes of me to sit in the North Stand

and pass judgement but it was becoming more and more obvious with each game that went by with Barnwell in charge, that the club were very likely to be finishing where it had been only a few months previous, ninety-second in the football league. Then I snapped.

16 December 1994. Black Friday.

On 16 December 1994 I witnessed the most awful game ever by a Cobblers' side. The bottom line was that for twenty-one years I had supported Northampton through thick and a great deal of thin but I just cannot recall a performance like the one that night. For me, the date you see above will go down in history as "Black Friday". That evening Northampton played a poor looking Scunthorpe United side. Scunthorpe looked tired, unimaginative and with little idea but Cobblers matched them in every department but one. Scunthorpe put their one clear cut chance away. We failed.

For me things were going wrong well before the game. In the warm-up period some thirty minutes before kick-off most of the Cobblers' team were warming up in front of the North Stand. I felt there seemed to be very little communication between players. Assistant manager Peter Morris could be seen mingling with some of the team. Martin Aldridge was receiving practice crosses which he was trying to slot away into the back of the net. Many he missed or totally miskicked. Although it meant nothing you could see his confidence was low, his head dropping. In the not too distant past I can remember previous Cobblers' managers taking a great deal of interest in the moments leading up to kick-off. Joe Kiernan for instance, would spend ages firing all sorts of shots at Peter Gleasure right up to the moment before kick-off. I remember commenting on this at the time. This meant that Gleasure's reactions were well and truly on the ball. (Unfortunately Mr Foley had other things planned for him.)

I could have got the wrong end of the stick here but I could not help but feel the preparation before the Scunthorpe game seemed wrong. In defence of the management I cannot see what goes on in the changing room. Five minutes into the game, I turned round to John and said,

"These are here for the taking."

Scunthorpe had played a gruelling FA Cup replay against high flying Birmingham City some forty-eight hours previous. It showed. For the first ten minutes Cobblers looked to have the game by the scruff of the neck until Scunthorpe scored a simple goal from a free kick. Nobody picked up the giant central defender Knill and his well placed header gave Stewart no chance. As far as I can remember that was the only shot on target Scunthorpe achieved in the entire ninety minutes.

From that moment on there was no way back for Cobblers. Like at Preston, against Swansea and again that night against Scunthorpe, a first half goal just killed us. When the header went in I turned round to John again and we both said the same thing.

"There is no way back now."

It was a ridiculous and negative statement. There were only ten minutes gone on my watch, but it proved to be correct. Almost immediately Cobblers forgot about a passing game and started pumping the ball straight up the middle of the park. These were easily dealt with by the six foot goodness-knows-what Knill. Those that the battered Trott managed to win went into deadman's space as Aldridge drifted in and mostly out of the game. The rest is history.

For some time I defended manager John Barnwell. Two weeks before this game I began to think that he had had enough time and things really must start to change. I wrote a short article in the "Chronicle & Echo". In spite of the title, "Back the Manager", which the "Chronicle & Echo" chose, this was not the point I was trying to get across. My point was, and still is, the vulgar and vocal criticism being thrown at Barnwell. Call me what you like but I could not join in with this. So we were left with two options:

1. The majority of fans view. John Barnwell, the man who took us to the bottom of the entire Football League for the first time ever, to go.

2. The Board's view. Mr Barnwell stays.

I was now in agreement with the majority. Both members of the then current management team had to go. When the final whistle went against Scunthorpe, skipper Ray Warburton could hardly bear to walk off he was so gutted. The following week I was going to Ireland for five days and would miss the next two games. I would have loved to have come back from County Kildare and seen that we had won both our games. If this had happened with Barnwell and Morris there, then fine. I would have held up my hands and said I was wrong.

Like Ray Warburton that night, I left Sixfields stunned. We could not blame the County Ground jinx any longer.

It later emerged that many other Northampton supporters had put pen to paper that night. The local press was swamped with correspondence. It appeared that 16 December 1994 was the straw that finally broke the camel's back for many loyal supporters.
On the evening of 29 December 1994, two days after Northampton had lost at home to Chesterfield, I returned home from County Kildare. By chance, I switched on the local news. Reports were breaking that John Barnwell had been sacked as manager of Northampton Town.

One thing I very rarely do is openly criticise a current manager of my club. As I said, support should be aimed at encouragement, not criticism. December 16 though was the last straw. John Barnwell had taken over from Phil Chard as manager the previous season. He had guided the Club to bottom place in the Football League for the first time in its history. At the start of the 1993/4 season he had made the usual pre-season signings. Some of these signings were good. However, other signings were somewhat puzzling. A strong emphasis had been put on non-league signings. One of these signings, Neil Grayson, proved a success. The previous season he had been voted Beazer Homes Premier Division player of the year whilst at Boston United. Others though were totally mystifying. Richard Skelly, Brett McNamara, Scott Middlemass, Mark Ovendale and Mark Turner for instance. With no disrespect to them they were simply nowhere near league standard. In fact, I will go as far as to say that some of the squad Barnwell had assembled would have struggled in the Conference.

December 16 was the culmination of a great deal of frustration, not just for me. Enough was enough.
There were many names linked to the now vacant hot seat at Sixfields. Vice Chairman, Barry Stonhill had been left with the task of facing the press after Barnwell's departure. Mr Stonhill went on record as saying that the Club would even welcome applications from some high profile ex-managers. Immediately the name of Ron Atkinson came to everybody's lips. In the cold light of day though, Mr Atkinson is a very charismatic and flamboyant figure. He is a terrific manager and there was very little chance of the Cobblers ever affording him. Many names cropped up but the Club said that it was not going to be rushed and took their time making the decision.

Whilst all this was going on off the pitch, Cobblers still played two league games with assistant manager Peter Morris in charge. Morris' name had also been linked to the Sixfields job. This filled many Cobblers' fans with fear. They felt that Morris was as much to blame for the slump in the team's fortune as Barnwell. Whether or not this was true, Morris did himself no favours at the New Year's Eve fixture at Darlington. Cobblers were totally humiliated in a 4-1 defeat at Feathams. It was a long way to go for New Year's Eve and the journey home down the Great North Road seemed a lot longer than it normally did. The atmosphere on the bus reminded me of the night coming back from Scunthorpe with the Conference staring us in the face.

The team's form was now getting so bad that if whoever came in as manager did not turn things round quickly, then Northampton would soon find themselves bottom of the entire league again. Surely the Club could not survive that humiliation again? The only things that made the day bearable in Darlington were the wonderful lunchtime stop at Richmond, which for me included a walk round the perimeter of the castle, the fish and chips, a pint of Strongarm and a consolation goal from Neil Grayson. The next match away at Wigan was Peter

Morris' last in charge. This also brought defeat. By now, on the terraces, there were two names being hotly tipped for the Cobblers' hotseat. One was ex-Rochdale manager Dave Sutton and the other Ian Atkins. Atkins had had brief spells in charge at Cambridge, Colchester and more recently Doncaster.

On January 10, after two weeks of waiting, the Club announced their decision. Ian Atkins had been appointed. I know that when speaking with Brian Lomax, he and many others had been very impressed with Atkins.

Atkins' impact on the Club was instant. He made two new signings within hours of his appointment. Darren Hughes from Port Vale and Chris Burns from Portsmouth. In his first game in charge at the Club, the Cobblers beat fellow strugglers Gillingham with two second half goals from Harmon (a penalty) and substitute Dean Trott in front of five and a half thousand spectators. When the referee blew the final whistle Atkins came onto the pitch to shake hands with his players. From three sides of the ground you could here the sighs of relief from the home supporters!

Cobblers had to wait two weeks before they played their next league game at home to Scarborough. Atkins had said there would be some lows as well as some highs and this game turned into an enormous low. Scarborough strolled away with a comfortable 3-0 win. Incredibly, there were just under six thousand spectators inside Sixfields for the game. With Scarborough's away following about the worst in the Football League, nearly all these fans were supporting the Cobblers. It showed that with the new stadium and a new young manager, incredible potential now existed at Northampton. Atkins had also appeared on the Anglia Television football programme "Kick Off". It was certainly very refreshing to see a manager of Northampton Town appearing live on the box in a positive fashion, not reminiscing about his golden days a decade previous.

Obviously there were still problems with the squad Atkins had inherited. All managers like to bring in their own men and Atkins was no exception. Over the next few weeks he brought in several new faces, the most noticeable being veteran striker Garry Thompson from Cardiff City, Nicky Smith a leftback on loan from non-league Sudbury, Andy Woodman a goalkeeper from Exeter City and Danny O'Shea, who was with Atkins at Cambridge United. Many of these, with the exception of Thompson, may not be household names but there was a lot of logic behind the new manager's thinking. Thompson for instance was no spring chicken but the experience he possessed proved invaluable and it soon started to rub off on younger members of the squad. In his debut against Preston which Cobblers won 2-1, Thompson's contribution was enormous. Certainly most of the North End players knew that Thompson had been on the park! He certainly left his mark on the game in more ways than one. When Atkins had signed Thompson he said that when you have him at your club, the first name the opposition look for on the team sheet before a game is Garry's! Smith was a revelation. In all he only played six games for the Cobblers, scoring one goal direct from a corner against Preston. For many Cobblers' fans though, his contribution to the season was immeasurable. Whilst he was at the Club in his loan period the Cobblers won two games and drew 4-4 in a cracking game at Craven Cottage against Fulham. Smith had a major part in these results. I understand that Atkins was very keen on signing Smith for much longer. Unfortunately he decided to go back into the non-league. The Woodman signing for me was the second biggest event in Cobblers' season after Atkins' appointment. All season Cobblers had had problems between the sticks. Billy Stewart, the number one choice, seemed to have little confidence. His understudy, Mark Ovendale cost the Cobblers many goals and points after a promising start. Things reached a head with the goalkeeping problem on March 4 away at Carlisle United. Ovendale started the game with Stewart on the bench. By half-time Cobblers were 2-0 down thanks mainly to a nightmare performance from Ovendale. As the second half kicked off a snowstorm had hit Cumbria. Sharron, John, Alison and I, who were staying up in the Lake District for the weekend, were covered in snow in no time. I had to remove my glasses because the snow was freezing to them! Billy Stewart was now in goal. Ovendale had been substituted and had played his last game for Northampton.

The next game was also a disaster. Without dwelling too much on events Cobblers were stuffed by Bury at Sixfields. After a fairly even first half, Northampton were blown away, mainly by David Pugh. The final result, 5-0 to Bury, did not do the away side's performance justice. It should have been more. It would have been interesting to see what Barnwell would have done in this situation. Atkins moved without a second thought. Stewart had also played his last game for the Cobblers. Four days later Northampton were fielding their third goalkeeper in as many games. Andy Woodman had been signed on a free from debt-ridden Exeter City. By all accounts Woodman's stay at St James Park had not been too happy. After spending seven seasons at Crystal Palace as number two to Nigel Martyn, Woodman had moved to Exeter only to be sent off twice in a very short space of time. He found himself side-lined as veteran goalkeeper, Peter Fox became first choice. In his first game for the Cobblers he dropped the first cross Rochdale put over. Fortunately the ball was cleared. That though, was his only error. For the rest of the game he caught everything and kept a clean sheet. In the away end we were all singing:

"A Cobblers' keeper's caught a cross, do dar, do dar!"

The 0-0 draw at Spotland after the Bury drubbing felt like a huge victory! It was noticeable that for the last ten games of the season with Woody in goal, Cobblers lost only two of them. Unfortunately one of these defeats came at Gigg Lane, Bury. Another 5-0 drubbing! Picture the scene. I've travelled up from Olney to Bury. I've watched my side get totally stuffed 5-0 for the second time in six weeks by the same side! I leave the ground and I'm sitting on the coach waiting for the long slog back down the M6. I'm thinking one thought and one thought only. Get this bus away from Gigg Lane, NOW! It is not so much the fact that I'm cheesed off at the 5-0 thrashing. It's everybody outside the bus looking in on us.

With one hand they show five fingers, then with the other hand they again show five fingers. Then both hands come up together with ten fingers showing! Even worse is that some of the individuals who are doing this are as young as five or six and they all seem to have the biggest grins spread over their faces! Bastards.

With Atkins' semi re-built squad, the season started to tail off satisfactorily. Whereas earlier on in the season heads dropped as soon as the opposition scored, there now appeared to be more spirit in the camp. In the dark days towards the end of Barnwell's era, the Club were not even picking up points. Now Northampton were managing to beat sides and to come from behind to secure points when all seemed lost. One of these points came near the end of the game away at Hartlepool when Garry Thompson managed to just force the ball over the line. It seemed to be the sheer presence of his bulk (and hand) that was the deciding factor! As Cobblers went into the penultimate game of the season, away at Barnet, the chances of them finishing bottom were now rarely talked about. Barring a freak set of results there was very little chance of Atkins' men finishing bottom. The game at Barnet was a classic. With well over a thousand Cobblers' fans present at Underhill, goals from Burns, Thompson and Warburton secured a famous 3-2 victory. At the final whistle the players came over to us and hundreds of hands were shaken. Atkins had achieved what he had set out to do. The impossible! After "Black Friday" I really thought the Cobblers would again finish bottom. Fortunately the Board had made the right decision and had appointed the right man.

Sharron and I had travelled down to Barnet by train. We got a lift back with John and Alison and ended up in "The Bull" at Newport Pagnell. A good night was had by all. The next Saturday, in all the hype of the Premiership, an extraordinary game against Exeter City went almost unnoticed.

It Went Almost Unnoticed.

It was no ordinary football game at the Sixfields Stadium, Northampton on 6 May 1995. In fact events off the field meant this game could well have been historic as the final nail was sinking into the Exeter coffin. The result on the pitch took a back seat as the raw emotion surrounding the afternoon took centre stage. For the record Northampton Town won 2-1. This lifted them to eighty-sixth place in the football league, their highest finish for four seasons. This may not sound like success but for the Club and its supporters this was almost like winning the FA Cup. When Exeter arrived at Sixfields on May 6 they were a possible twelve days away from extinction. The bottom line was that they needed to find £350,000 before May 18. Exeter's estimated total debt differed slightly depending on what source one heard it from. The general belief was that it stood at £1.4 million. The future was looking bad for Exeter. May 6 looked like being their last game ever. As a result nearly a thousand of their supporters travelled up to Northampton to witness the possible last rights on their club. For the true football supporter just think what this must be like.

There were nearly six thousand Northampton supporters at the game so in total the gate was just short of seven thousand. Before the game Northampton Director, Brian Lomax made a public announcement to the Exeter supporters wishing them all the best and never to give up hope. This was welcomed from the travelling supporters in the South Stand. When the half-time whistle went, some Exeter fans unveiled a large banner saying,

"DON'T LET OUR CITY DIE!"

This was widely applauded by all the Northampton supporters. If anyone should know what they were going through then, it was them! Many of the home supporters were also singing,

"Don't let City die!"

Things really started to get emotional when the final whistle went. Hundreds of Exeter supporters ran onto the pitch and gathered in front of the main stand. Many made their way towards the Northampton end. The reaction of the home supporters to this pitch invasion was incredible. Spontaneous applause and cheering broke out. The home fans started singing the name of Exeter. Several Northampton fans also decided to invade the pitch and met the Exeter fans head on. What then happened hardly received a mention anywhere on television or in the press. Rival football supporters met face to face on the pitch and started to hug each other, shake hands, shed tears and swap scarves. Many football tops were also swapped. The pitch was a sea of not just claret but also red and white. Some Exeter fans were totally numbed. One fan sat inconsolable with his red and white flag in the centre circle. The police were nowhere to be seen. I have seen many scenes and emotions at football matches but I have never seen anything like this before. We will probably never know what the true extent of Exeter's awful financial predicament and what the reasons for it were. A sad fact is that six months wages of a top Premier League player would have saved Exeter an awful headache.

By beating Exeter three important things had happened. Atkins had secured two back to back league wins for the first time in fourteen months. This meant that Cobblers finished ten points off the bottom. The win had also left Exeter stranded at the bottom of the entire league just to add to their problems.

1995/1996

West Bromwich Albion.

Supporting a Third Division club does have some drawbacks. One of these is that some of the grounds we regularly travel to are not the most salubrious. At the time of writing I have attended sixty of the ninety-two league grounds. Nearly all the grounds I have done are in the lower Divisions. I have lost count of the number of times I have been to Mansfield, Brentford or Cardiff, but at the time of writing I have never attended Old Trafford, Anfield or Elland Road.

So, can you imagine how excited I was when the Cobblers were drawn away to First Division West Bromwich Albion in the first round of the Coca Cola Cup. The Hawthorns was an unvisited ground. Another good thing about this midweek draw was that West Brom is an away ground I could get to without having to take a half day annual leave. Sharron and I finished work in Milton Keynes at 16:45 and made our way over to John and Alison's in Hunsbury. Just after seven o'clock John was pulling off junction 1 of the M5 with The Hawthorns only about a quarter of a mile off. It could not have been any easier. Parking was not a problem as right opposite the ground was "Bradford's Bakery". For £1, supporters could use their staff car park. With Alison expecting, this could not have been more convenient.

Knowing that I had a long night ahead of me, I had gorged myself in the staff canteen at lunchtime. Sharron however, was slightly more hungry. Bang next door to the ground was a posh looking mobile food outlet with chips painted all over it. She made her way over only to discover that they in fact did not sell chips!! When we had entered the ground Sharron feasted on a packet of crisps and a Twix. The crisps cost an astonishing 55p!

I had been slightly mystified on my way up to the Hawthorns not to have seen any claret and white scarves on show. Even some twenty minutes before kick-off there seemed very few visible outside of the ground. This surprised me as Birmingham is only an hour from Northampton. As soon as we arrived in the ground the reason became apparent. They were already there! As we made our way into the stadium my vision was immediately filled with bright colours. Opposite was a large new stand with "Apollo 2000" on the roof. This stand was filled with thousands of blue seats, hundreds of which were occupied with supporters wearing the traditional striped West Brom tops and many others who adorned the yellow away strips. As we made our way up the stairs to the stand, the pitch came into view. In spite of the worst drought in three hundred years, the pitch had to be the best I have ever seen. It had obviously been well-watered and was a lush, deep green, unlike my back lawn which was covered in dying brown grass. To add to this, most of the Northampton fans adorned their claret tops.

The previous season, the Cobblers suffered the humiliation of two 5-0 defeats at the hands of Bury. Four days previous, on the opening day of the season, they had thumped Bury 4-1 at Sixfields. I know that you cannot judge a team on just one performance, but the way in which Bury had been blown away had given supporters a rare bit of optimism. Was Ian Atkins living up to the promise he had shown at the start of his spell in charge of the Club at the end of last season? An away fixture at First Division West Brom would be as big a test as you could want. I settled down for the next ninety minutes. Before the Bury game I had still been in cricket season mode. Within two minutes of the start, my football appetite was once again rushing through my veins. Arriving at such a superb venue as The Hawthorns I was now in one hundred per cent football mode, in spite of the oppressive, hot weather. As the teams were poised for kick-off I could hardly contain myself. It took only a few minutes to realise that the Bury performance was not a flash in the pan. Gone were the days when Cobblers' midfield seem to be outnumbered in height and ability. Burns, O'Shea and Peer, as on Saturday, began to dominate proceedings. Let me not take anything away from West Brom. Apart from their leftback, who was having a nightmare, they looked a good side. They put some good, slick passing movements together but for once the Cobblers matched them.

On forty-one minutes, the most surprising thing of the entire evening happened, West Brom scored. In the end it was a slick move that broke down the stubborn Cobblers defence and the prolific Bob Taylor buried a close range header. As the side had shown in the last two matches of the previous season, they would not lie down and die. There appeared to be a new spirit in the team. Heads did not drop. The second half commenced and the midfield once again started to orchestrate things. I sat there in the stand just about purring. I was enjoying the game so much that I did not want it to end. I hardly cared how long was to go. I was just enthralled at a Cobblers' side playing with such commitment. Although small by West Brom standards, the crowd of nearly seven thousand helped as well. The atmosphere was electric with the away support hardly relenting for the entire ninety minutes. On seventy-one minutes the expected happened. The fast improving Lee Colkin robbed a Baggies defender on the half way line and powered forward. As he entered the penalty area he seemed to miskick the ball. As the home fans cheered and gesticulated at him, a defender left the ball thinking the goalkeeper had it covered. As the ball harmlessly ran between them, Colkin continued his run and poked the ball into the corner of the net with the defender and the goalkeeper looking at each other. What a moment! I went berserk as Colkin lapped up his moment of glory. Never before did a Cobblers' goal seem more deserved.

With about ten minutes left West Brom made a double substitution. The two fresh pairs of legs made a big difference and the Cobblers' defence was stretched. Throughout the game, the biggest threat to the Cobblers had been from their ex-player Dave Gilbert. With the last kick of the game, he threaded his way through the defence and fired the ball towards the corner of the net only to see Andy Woodman, at full stretch, tip it round the post. Seconds later, in an excellently refereed game, the final whistle was blown. A classic game and one I will always remember. If I had been a Baggies supporter I would have been stunned beyond belief. Perpetual basement strugglers Northampton, two Divisions below us, walkover. On this night however, things were different. Cobblers were equal to just about everything West Brom threw at them.

On the way back down the M6, in the cold light of the day, I reckon this was the best performance I had seen by a Cobblers' side since the record breaking days of 1986/87.

By the time Sharron and I arrived home in Olney, the church was striking midnight. It had been a long day. We had left Olney some sixteen hours earlier, done a full day's work, gone to West Bromwich via Northampton, seen the game and then made our way home. Arriving home we had a very late tea, washed up and finally clambered into bed at one o'clock. Tired we may have been, content, very. Yes, it was early days yet but I was dreaming claret and white shirts flowing forward before my head had touched the pillow.

It was only the first leg though!

(In the second leg WBA left Sixfields with a 4-2 win under their belt.)

Hartlepool away 29.8.95

The things you do!

When the fixture list for the 1995/6 season came out, the Cobblers were given three midweek away league fixtures. The league had done us proud in one of these fixtures, Cambridge United, only about fifty miles from Northampton. The other two though were somewhat mystifying: Hartlepool and Exeter! Why they could not have used a bit of common sense and given us midweek games at the nearer fixtures like Barnet, Fulham or Leyton Orient puzzles me no end. Even worse was on the evening of 12 September, Torquay had to travel up to Hartlepool!

On August 30 I got married. Sharron and I had decided on the date and time some eight months earlier, before the 1995/6 fixtures were anywhere near being thought about! When they were published in the July, there in black and white, on the evening before I was due to be married was Hartlepool away! Without a second thought, I immediately ruled out any possibility of seeing the game. We had planned a small wedding, no big fuss, none of the "you must not see the dress beforehand", "you must be apart the night before" lark. In fact, I went to okay the dress for Sharron and most of the family were going to join us at home the night before. Very untraditional, yes, but that was the way we wanted it.

A few days before the Hartlepool game, John and I were discussing whether or not he was going to go up. In spite of the very late arrival home and the long day following, he said he was going. Then Sharron said to me,

"Well do you want to go then? You're more than welcome."

So, to cut a long story short, I ended up booking my seat on the coach, along with a guest appearance from my life long mate Darren "Chunky" Panter.

The Monday of that week was a Bank Holiday. When I woke up that morning I knew I had a knackering three days ahead of me. It started on that evening as friends and family met up in Olney Working Men's Club for a quite drink and get together. By the end of the evening as we made our way home I totted up how many pints of Guinness I had consumed. Nearly a gallon of Guinness. Now I'm not a great drinker, I know my limits and seven pints of Guinness is a lot for me. The strange thing was that walking home along the High Street I felt stone-cold sober. With the house full of relatives I ended up sleeping up in the loft extension on a blow up camp bed! Not the most comfortable of night's sleep. On the morning of the Hartlepool game I walked down the High Street in Olney before setting out to catch the bus from Sixfields. It was then that the aftermath of the night before hit me. I felt very hungover and tender! It did not wear off.

Chunk and I arrived at Sixfields at about half past one after picking John up from West Hunsbury. Thankfully I had brought some Nurofen and as the coach reached the A1, I succumbed as a new and improved hammer started to inflict its damage on my already tender head. We made very good time up to the North East and arrived on the outskirts of Hartlepool at half past five. By this time, John and Chunk had become thirsty. I, however, felt no inclination to participate in any liquid refreshment whatsoever. Unknown to us the steward of the coach had already booked a stopping off point in advance. Extra food and staff had been laid on. This was a wise move on their part as not one but two coach loads of Cobblers' fans arrived at his door. Entering the bar I still could not face anything too heavy in the way of drink and opted for a pint of weak shandy. Meanwhile John and Chunk were having a great time as they found an exceptional hand pump ale from the other bar. After a couple of these they thought it might be wise to go on to the halves as the night was still young. In the meantime, I was becoming very sad. I was still slowly making my way through my first pint of shandy! Their decision to go on to the halves backfired somewhat. As the time for us to board the coach approached three more very quick halves of hand pump were squeezed in. Knowing John well, I thought his decision to visit the gents on his way out was very prudent thinking.

It was only five months previous that John and I had been to the Victoria Ground. In early April their new stand along one side of the pitch seemed a long way from being completed. Now in late August it was completed with fans actually seated in it. Even more astonishing for us was the end where we had been put in April. Then, about two-thirds of this concrete bank seemed to have been condemned. The other third, seemed to be set aside for travelling supporters and to be totally honest, was a complete insult to anyone who had made the effort to travel to Hartlepool.

Now in August, this end was totally unrecognisable with a new roofed terrace stand there. John and I were totally amazed at the transformation. Hartlepool had certainly pulled its finger and had improved its ground immeasurably.

Unfortunately they do not seem to be able to get the crowds to even remotely fill it. The official attendance that night was just over two thousand three hundred. This somewhat surprised us as there barely looked much more than about one thousand two hundred there. The travelling away support had once again done Northampton proud. In all, three coaches had made the long trip north and there must have been about three hundred fans in the away end. By the time the game started, John and Chunk were pretty merry. I suppose this was not a bad thing as the first half was a very sobering affair with both sides showing very little imagination.

Suddenly, out of nothing, Hartlepool attacked down the left. A hopeful cross came over but there was no Pools forward on the receiving end. Then the nightmare happened. As the ball made its way over to the far post, fullback Darren Hughes had one of those moments that he will want to forget for the rest of his life! As he turned to run away with the ball it seemed to hit him on the back of his legs and squeezed in at the far post beating a helpless and stunned Andy Woodman. A freak goal and certainly one that took the stuffing out the vocal away support. Over two hundred miles up to the North East to see that! Cobblers went into half-time still one nil down. Immediately after half-time Atkins made a double substitution, it later emerged that they were made out of necessity. Grayson was suffering from hamstring trouble whilst Hughes, unknown to us, had suffered what was later described by many as the worst dislocation ever seen to his thumb.

Atkins must have dished out one heck of a rocketing at half-time because Cobblers took control right from the kick-off. They pressured the Pools goal and were very soon rewarded when substitute Garry Thompson let fly with a bullet header that hit the back of the net almost before Horne could move. The away following had been pretty vocal all night but now they really erupted. From then on it was one-way traffic as claret and white shirts pushed forward in a bid to get the second goal. As time went on they could just not break down the stubborn Pools defence and with about fifteen minutes to go Cobblers visibly started to wilt. The tables were turned and Cobblers were forced onto the back foot and desperately defended. As the final whistle approached Cobblers were camped in their own half. I turned to John and Chunk,

"We are going to be lucky to hold out here."

Eighty-nine minutes were showing on my stopwatch as Pools won a free kick just inside the Cobblers' half. As the ball was struck into the penalty area Woodman was beaten to the ball by Henderson and he headed in. Well that's football for you. It does not matter whether the winning goal is scored in the first or ninetieth minute, it counts. It just seems a bit more cruel when you have travelled all that way on a Tuesday night only to lose to a last minute goal! Before the Hartlepool celebrations had begun to die down the referee had blown up and that was that. It was at about this time that I realised that I had finally sobered up from the night before! We clambered aboard our coach rather subdued and left Hartlepool at 21:35 with a long haul still ahead of us. As we passed Middlesborough I managed to ring Sharron on John's mobile phone. I estimated that I would be home at about 01:30. I should have known better! The coach trundled on south untroubled until we reached Nottingham where an accident caused us to be delayed for nearly forty minutes. We arrived back at Sixfields just before 01:30. I dropped John off at Hunsbury, then Chunk in Stoke Goldington, arriving back in Olney at 02:10 on the morning of my wedding!

Nine hours later, back in Northampton we were married followed by the reception in Olney. Sixteen hours after I arrived home from Hartlepool we were on our way to Shannon Airport in the Republic of Ireland. For our first night of marriage we stopped in Newmarket-on-Fergus, County Clare. It had been a long but extremely pleasurable forty-eight hours. As we had a meal before we made our way back to our room in the "Hunter's Lodge", I decided to brave a pint of Irish Guinness. I was rewarded with the most delicious pint of the black liquid I had ever tasted. As it was my wedding night I refrained from another! The things you do!

Another Day, Another Dollar, Doncaster 1995.

Some of you reading this may be used to following your top flight clubs to the likes of Old Trafford, White Hart Lane and Elland Road, week in, week out. Every now and again you may be drawn against a Darlington or a Scarborough in the Cup. The real bread and butter of the Football League.

In the last few years football stadia have started to change beyond all recognition. The City Ground in Nottingham, Molineaux in Wolverhampton and Anfield, home of Liverpool, now have upgraded stadia that are only bettered by a few of the top Italian clubs. Following Northampton every week, I very rarely see these grounds except on "Match of the Day". Unless the Cobblers have a couple of highly successful years, the only time I will visit these stadia will be if they for once in a blue moon were to get into the third round of the FA Cup or the second round of the League Cup! So, for eight months of the year, every other Saturday is spent travelling to Third Division grounds. And yes, I do have a great time and yes, I would like to visit some more rather exotic stadia. However, at the moment it looks like the only way I am going to see the Old Traffords of this world is if the Cobblers are not playing and I attend one of these grounds as a neutral.

So reading this you may just have come back from Liverpool v Blackburn. You almost certainly saw an action packed game in front of over thirty thousand fans in one of the most spectacular re-vamped stadia in England. Where was I? Well on the day that Liverpool did play Blackburn at Anfield I was at probably the most contrasting ground in the whole of the football league, Belle Vue, Doncaster. Until September 1995, I had never been to Belle Vue. It is one of the grounds that Northampton regularly play at but for a variety of different reasons I had never managed to see a game there. With Halifax going out of the league and with the Cobblers moving out of the dilapidated County Ground I would have reckoned that Darlington probably had the worst ground in the football league, that was until I turned up at Doncaster. This is not meant as a criticism of that club or of Darlington come to that. As I have explained on many occasions, being a supporter of Northampton Town meant constant embarrassment with our ground until we were lucky enough to move to Sixfields. I am not singling out Doncaster, Halifax or Darlington, they are just examples. Northampton were fortunate to have a very positive local Council elected with a new community stadium being top of their manifesto. What clubs like Darlington or Doncaster would give to have that Council like that, goodness only knows.

I was told by several people that facilities for travelling supporters had improved no end at Doncaster. It was the case that away fans were herded into a section of terrace which was enclosed in a type of cage! This day though the away fans had been given what was left of a terrace behind one of the goals. This, by all accounts, was a vast improvement. I stood just behind the right of the goal and took in the view of the ground. The opposite terrace at the North end of the ground was small and, like the away end, was completely open to the elements. On the right-hand side of the pitch stood the old and antiquated looking stand. Its length was around half that of the pitch. The middle section of the stand seemed to be taped off rather like a murder scene. It looked like someone had recently tried to set light to it. To each side of this stand was a small section of open terracing. Opposite the stand and to our left was another section of terracing. This terrace again ran along only about three-quarters of the length of the pitch and only seemed to be partially covered by a small roof. This meant that a large corner of the ground to our left was an unoccupied piece of grass bank. The end result of what I have described meant that about two-thirds of the ground was completely open to the elements. That day, Cobblers had taken around five or six hundred supporters to Doncaster. As kick-off approached many tried to start singing to encourage the team. With none of the away end and most of the ground open to the elements, the noise created just vanished into thin air. To this day I will never know if the home supporters tried to sing or motivate Rovers. They appeared to make no noise at all. Coupled with the spacious and open nature of the ground the entire proceedings seemed to be devoid of any atmosphere.

On the stroke of half-time and against the run of play, the only goal of the game was scored. The Doncaster goalkeeper, Perry Suckling pumped the ball up the park and well into the Northampton half. Ian Sampson headed the ball clear and it fell to Rovers number eight Brabin who hit it first time on the volley and past Andy Woodman from nearly thirty yards. A goal out of nothing but a class piece of finishing. The Northampton supporters were not too impressed with this and a deathly hush ensued. The strange thing was that in spite of just taking the lead, the goal hardly seemed to make a difference to the home fans. There was a bit cheering, some hand clapping and a muffled chorus of,

"You're not singing any more!"

Then life seemed to go on as normal. Was it me or was I imagining it but Doncaster hardly seemed to get enthusiastic about scoring? In the months leading up to this game I know that Doncaster had been desperate to get away from Belle Vue. Until you actually see their problems at first hand, one does not realise what an uphill struggle they have. With the divide between the Premier League and the smaller clubs getting wider, clubs like Doncaster Rovers are going to find it more and more difficult to survive. It does not matter how good their team is or what success it achieves, their ground will always be a liability. I do not wish to rub Doncaster's nose in it because supporting Northampton we had to put up with a pigsty for years and then utter embarrassment after our stand was pulled down after the Bradford fire. I really hope that they can sort out their problems. I obviously do not know the true extent of what they are up against as I am not privy to what is going on but unless it is resolved quickly Doncaster Rovers could well find themselves in oblivion. I, for one, would hate to see that.

Moving House.

Moving house is always a stressful time. When I sold my property in January 1996 I was very lucky. The funny thing is that I remember all the significant dates by when the Cobblers were playing!

It all started on January 13. I had just been shopping at the Coop and was sitting down in front of the television to watch "Football Italia" on Channel Four. Sharron was due back from aerobics at any time. As the programme commenced, I started supping my cup of tea and Sharron came in from aerobics. An ordinary Saturday morning in Olney when Cobblers are playing at home. No sooner had Sharron uttered the words,

"I'm just going to have a quick bath",

than the doorbell rang. There stood the estate agent with a couple standing behind him.

"Quentin, we were just passing when we saw your notice in the window. Do you mind if I show this couple round? If not we can always come back later."

I could see no point in turning anybody away, so I said:

"Of course Steve, show them round."

At this point I apologised for the mess everywhere. If I have to be honest the house probably looked the most untidy it had ever been. Before going to aerobics Sharron had stripped the bed. The duvet and pillows were in a heap. There was washing all over the radiators. We had not had time to hoover for well over a week. The night before I had been working on the PC. There were books, discs, articles and a briefcase lying all over the dining table. The breakfast things were all stacked up in the kitchen. There was also a pile of drying up on the draining board. We rarely live in such a tip, but on this morning the place looked like a bomb had landed! As the agent was showing the couple round, Sharron postponed her bath until they had finished. As we looked around the chaos of the lounge I thought there was absolutely no way this couple would be interested. It was only the fact that they had seen the details I had put in the front window that they had, on the off chance, decided to look round. In all I suppose they were there about a quarter of an hour. When they had left Sharron had her bath while I went and washed up. Almost immediately we forgot that they had ever turned up. Even when we had some forewarning that viewers were going to turn up and the place looked clean, we had had very little interest.

I was eating my lunch just after one o'clock. In another forty-five minutes we would be heading off towards Sixfields for the Cardiff game. The telephone rang. I thought it would be Fred or George confirming the travel arrangements. I was wrong. It was the estate agent. Another viewing I thought? What he actually said was:-

"Hello Quentin. The couple I brought round this morning, they loved the place and have put an offer in already!"

I sat there on the chair speechless. It was totally unexpected. Things soon started to happen. Firstly Cobblers beat Cardiff City in one of the best games ever seen at Sixfields. Cobblers played the last twenty-five minutes with only ten men after goalkeeper Andy Woodman had been sent off for handling outside the area. Midfielder Chris Burns came off the bench and went between the sticks. When the final whistle went, the Cobblers' win meant that they had in fact done the treble over Cardiff! (Afterwards, Kenny Hibbett, the Cardiff manager, stated that he still thought that Cardiff were the better side.)

In the days after the Cardiff game, we agreed a price on our house and started to look for a new place. Buying and selling houses is said to be the most stressful time in life apart from close bereavements. For us though it could not have been easier. We had first time buyers and we had agreed, so as not to jeopardise the sale, that we would move into my parents' before the sale on our new place had been arranged. This meant that there was no chain involved. Because our buyers had a one hundred per cent mortgage we exchanged and completed on the same day. I know the date because it was the day before Plymouth Argyle away! Two days before the game, we both had the day of work to move out of Newton Street. In spite of already moving a great deal of stuff up to my Mum and Dad's loft, it took five of us until six o'clock in the evening to move nearly everything out. By that time we were totally exhausted. Both Sharron and I had been up until 01:00 that morning sorting stuff out!

Our night had not finished there. After my Mum had made us a curry for tea we were back down to Newton Street to sort the last bits and pieces out. To cut a long story short it was 23:30 when we finally sat down. Then there was the problem of the cat! By the time I got out of bed at 06:30 on the Friday morning to sort out the rubbish still in the back garden I had managed about four hours sleep! It was a fraught night with the cat! At this stage in proceedings, I was in two minds about the Plymouth game. Both of us were in desperate need of some rest, sleep and a quiet day on the Saturday to refill our tanks. On the other hand, a trip down to Devon could have been just what the doctor ordered. It would take our minds off everything, so we decided to go. When I had sorted the rubbish out in the garden at Newton Street that Friday morning there were just two small jobs left. I read the meters and wheeled the barbecue through the streets of Olney to my Mum and Dad's. That was it. We were out of our house. The sale was completed that morning whilst we were at work. That night, on the eve of the Plymouth game, both Sharron and I were too tired to think about cooking tea. Instead we strolled down to our favourite Chinese restaurant on the Market Square and feasted there.

Needless to say I slept like a log that night until the fraught cat woke me up at 05:30. The next thing I knew was the alarm going off at 06:45. We both struggled out of bed and headed off towards Sixfields to catch the bus for Plymouth. Supporting Northampton does have its benefits. Its location is fairly central which is handy when travelling to away games. As we passed Bristol, Plymouth was still a long way off. Northampton to Plymouth seems like a never-ending journey to me. You would have to be really dedicated to follow the Pilgrims home and away from Devon. Some of the trips to the North East must take eight or nine hours. Added to that must be the expense of it all. I would have loved to have switched the alarm off that morning, rolled over and gone back to sleep. I had calculated that, in the three days leading up to the Plymouth game, it was unlikely that my total number of hours sleep had reached double figures. It was a strange thing that day. Although I desperately wanted to stay at our temporary home and unwind I felt that I just could not miss the game. There were two reasons for this. First and foremost was the usual fact that I would have felt the shame and guilt of missing the match. Although I was moaning about getting out of bed so early, I would have whinged ever more if I had been stuck in front of the telly waiting for the result to appear on the teleprinter! The second big reason why I had to go was that Home Park was a ground that I had not visited. It was number fifty-nine completed out of the ninety-two.

At long last the bus arrived at Home Park. There was a good turnout of travelling fans there. We met up with John who was down there with Alison and young Miss Whelan, along with many others, for the weekend.

"How are your vibes?" he asked.
"Not so good," I replied.

Sometimes it can be strange before games. Sometimes I can almost sense whether it will be our day or not. On other occasions I can walk into Sixfields and the atmosphere is good. Other times it can be uncertain and then it can be worse, the atmosphere can be quiet and tense, like people know that things are going to be a struggle and to expect the worse. This may sound a load of old tosh, but often the vibes I get turn out to be true. As I've said, my vibes at Plymouth were not so good. I put this down to the fact that I had been stuck on a bus since half past eight that morning and was dog tired more than anything else.

Cobblers had played Plymouth twice already in the season. On both occasions they had beaten them 1-0 at Sixfields, once in the League and once in the Auto Windscreens Shield. For the Auto Windscreens game Plymouth had fielded a near on reserve side but for the League game they had all but dominated the game only to lose to an Ian Sampson strike in the first half. As soon as the game kicked off at Home Park the game fell into the pattern of the last meeting at the Home of Football. Cobblers could hardly get the ball from the Pilgrims. Plymouth played a good passing game, very patient and with very few long ball hoofs. From the first minute Cobblers, without skipper "Razor" Ray Warburton, were on the back foot. Fortunately for us, a combination of poor finishing and good goalkeeping from Andy Woodman kept them out. O'Shea and Sampson at the back were rock solid and the lethal Adrian Littlejohn hardly touched the ball. And that was the pattern of play for the rest of the game apart from a moment of panic in the Plymouth defence as Jason White broke free only to see his shot hit the post and come out. With seven minutes left the deadlock was broken in a comical fashion. After a tussle in the goalmouth the ball broke to Micky Evans who went to fire the ball into the back of the net. To sum up the whole afternoon he completely miskicked the ball. It seemed to bounce up off his thigh. As the ball landed it appeared to spin over the goalline. A complete fluke! (Television pictures later confirmed this.)

A goal is a goal though. The reaction from a hundred or so Plymouth supporters who were sitting just to the right of the Cobblers' end was instantaneous. They all piled down the terrace towards us gesticulating in rather an unfriendly manner! It was pretty provocative. There were plenty of fences and stewards between us and them but at one point tempers were starting to get fraught. The stewards were obviously used to this section of the home "fans". There were double the amount of uniforms there than anywhere else in the ground. On the front of their fluorescent jackets was printed the name of the security company by whom they were employed. To be honest, I am always very sceptical of private security companies inside football grounds and this day backed up my feelings. There always seems to be some kind of problem when they are around. At Home Park there had been a handful of little incidents that really should have been stopped straightaway. Before the game and during half-time the Exeter speedway team were riding around the touch line. Every time they went passed this section of the crowd, many stood up to hurl insults, which is fair enough as I don't think Exeter are too popular in Plymouth, but a tiny minority seemed to take a great dislike to the rider in the black leathers. Every time he rode past them, this minority stood up and hurled coins at him. On one occasion, we could hear the coins connecting with his crash helmet. If one of these had got inside his visor he would have ended up in all sorts of bother. What did the uniforms do? Absolutely nothing.

When Plymouth had scored and they had all raced over to the Cobblers' end I certainly saw several coins flying in our direction. Again nobody was hauled out. A very small number of Cobblers' fans angered by this made their way over to the fence. You can almost guess what happened. The uniforms escorted one of the Cobblers' fans from the ground. One uniform had a vice-like grip on the supporter's wrist. This obviously troubled many ordinary Cobblers' fans and I immediately started thinking of civil liberties and what right that steward had to handle the supporter in that fashion. Unlike the terrific stewards at Mansfield a month before, these from Plymouth hardly spoke to any of us. Many seemed to glare at us as if we were in the way and to be honest many of them looked as though they had been recruited from the worst of the West Country's night-clubs.

For the final few minutes, Plymouth played good possession football and Cobblers could hardly get the ball from them. The game ended with Plymouth now strengthening their push for outright promotion. The Cobblers' fans were kept behind! When we were finally let out, not through the entrance we had come but along the main home terrace, not one steward said a good-bye. Many just seemed to stare! I've got nothing against Plymouth but certainly the stewards they employ need a lesson in public relations!

Sharron and I said good-bye to John and settled down the best we could on the coach. I hate travelling in cars and can't settle in them. Coaches I find a little easier. It is rare that I sleep on them but on this day it was no surprise that I remembered nothing between Weston-Super-Mare and Avonmouth. We really could have done without the long journey just after moving house but it just had to be done. In the cold light of the day, Cobblers really didn't deserve much out of the game. Thankfully for me, losing was not the end of the world. Although we were gripped with play-off fever it was a refreshing change to travel all the way down to deepest Devon knowing that a loss would not mean another look at the top of the Conference table. After four years of struggle, it takes some adjusting to! We finally arrived back at my Mum and Dad's in Olney at 22:20. After the events of the previous week and that day, I have to admit that I have never felt so tired in all my life as that night. It was not so much a feeling of tiredness but of total exhaustion. I don't know what state we looked in when we came through the back door but the first words my Mum said were,

"Would you like a cup of tea and some vegetable soup?"

When we sat down to eat, it tasted out of this world. I was so tired that I did not even watch "Match of the Day". The next thing I knew was at half past nine the next morning.

Deepdale.

There I was standing at the bar an hour before the away game at Exeter. John and Simon were with me. As is the norm talk was solely football. There's a surprise! Big Dave who runs the Trust Travel Club found his way over to us. He must have been waiting in the wings for us to hit our third and last pint before he came out with his now famous remark! Addressing John and I he said,

"Now here are a couple of responsible people."

I was choking in my Draught Flowers. In all fairness Dave did not beat round the bush and soon came to the point.

"Do you two fancy stewarding the bus to Preston? The Trust are running a bus up to Blackpool on the weekend of the Preston game. We need some bodies to help run a bus on the day as normal from Northampton."

And that was about that. Both John and I were roped into running the bus to Preston.

Six and a bit weeks later, on the morning of the match, I found myself heading towards Sixfields to help run the bus with John. Eight months earlier the Supporters Trust had decided to start running another bus to away games. This now meant that for the 1995/6 season the supporters of Northampton Town had three different travel organisations running buses for away games. Not bad for a Third Division club. I had travelled with the other two over the years, first with the Mounties and then with the St James Bus (known as the Jimmies End Bus). I had stopped travelling with the Mounties because on several occasions the quality of buses had been very poor and had reached several grounds late, half-time at Fulham for instance! The Jimmies End I had no real problem with. The only complaint I had with them was that at times it seemed like half the folk on the bus were smoking. As a non-smoker there can be nothing worse than this. I know there have been times when I have arrived home after using the Jimmies End bus reeking of tobacco smoke. A minor point though. When Dave Linnell announced the formation of the Trust Travel Club I thought I would give it a go.

One of Dave's reasons for forming the Travel Club was to open up a new source of additional funds to be ploughed straight back into the Supporters Trust and ending up directly in the pocket of the Club. Another reason he wanted to run a bus was that he thought that many supporters were put off away travel by the quality of the buses already available from the other travel clubs. The Trust Travel Club wanted to offer luxury coaches that guaranteed a video, toilet and hot drinks to the paying customer. As a result of this, many supporters and other individuals who travelled on rival buses started referring to the Trust Bus as the "Posh Bus"! Many of the supporters who used the Trust Bus had not defected from the other travel clubs. An entirely new clientele had sprung up. Many fans who had not previously travelled to away games started to use the Trust Bus. There were, of course, teething problems. The Trust were concerned as to the quality of some of the buses the coach company were supplying. They did not always come up to the standard requested, which of course was one of the reasons the Trust Travel Club had been formed. On the whole though, the first season of running the "Posh Bus" proved to be a great success. Certainly Sharron, John and I were more than happy. It was also a comfort to know that any profit the bus made went directly back into the Trust and hence into the coffers of the Cobblers. This was borne out in early 1996 when Ali Gibb was signed from Norwich City in a deal which cost Northampton £30,000. In the fantasy world of the Premier League sums like this come as a snip to clubs. In Division Three in 1996, this is a great deal of money and takes some finding. In the Ali Gibb signing £1,138 of profit from running the Trust Bus was given over to the Club to help secure his signature.

So, on the morning of April 13, I found myself helping to steward this bus to Preston. I met up with John at 09:20 outside Sixfields. The bus turned up at the same time as me. I could tell John was apprehensive. Dave had dropped off the up-to-date list of the bookings at John's just before he set off with his coach load up to Blackpool for the weekend. We were only two short of a full coach. Ten minutes before we were due to set off, I decided to have a count up. We were four people short, all from the same family. I know there has been nothing worse for Dave and his crew than when individuals who book up on the bus fail to turn up. It had happened on quite a few occasions when there had been a full bus booked and Dave had been turning people away. It is annoying to think that people can be so nonchalant about such things. At the end of the day they are costing the Trust and thereby the Club money they would otherwise have received. At one minute to ten I looked at my watch and said,

"They have got a minute to get here."

Ten o'clock came. John made his way on to the coach with Sharron. I was following on behind when a car load of folks came round the corner and parked up. It was our family of four with seconds to spare! They clambered aboard and soon the coach was heading on its way up the M6 towards Lancashire.

There are several tasks that have to be performed when running a supporters coach. One of the biggest fell to Sharron who had been volunteered in her absence. Running the shop. Other tasks which John and I had to carry out were the collecting of the money, organising a draw card, sorting out the video and collecting the rubbish. This may not sound like a lot but it certainly made the journey up to Preston pass quickly! Unfortunately there were major roadworks on the M6 junction of the M62. As we crawled slowly through this the B-Team bus stewards realised that the pub stop that Dave had pre-arranged was going to be somewhat curtailed. Coupled with this, reports indicated that a very large crowd was expected at Deepdale as Preston were on the verge of outright promotion into the Second Division. We were going to have to leave the pub early as well.

Thankfully we arrived in one piece at Deepdale with time to spare before kick-off. I have been to Preston five times now. On each occasion I have been put in a different part of the stadium! Preston had decided to put us opposite the terrific new "Tom Finney Stand". It was certainly very impressive which is more than can be said of the bit of terrace the travelling away fans had been given. Even worse was the state of the toilets. (By full time they were ankle deep in urine and supporters were having memories of Swansea.) By kick-off, our little area was packed with Cobblers' fans. Many others were seated behind us in the stand. Because of our position, I could not see one of them! Another terrific turnout.

As I have already said, at this time in April 1996, Preston were on the verge of promotion. They had only lost four games all season. Coupled with this, Preston manager, Gary Peters had just spent £200,000 on the prolific Gary Bennett from Tranmere Rovers. This added to their strong attacking line up which also included Andy Saville who had been hitting the target with consistency all season. I had turned up at Deepdale expecting one of two things. Either Cobblers would get a good hammering or they would cause a major shock. In the week leading up to the game, I have to confess that in spite of all the odds stacked against us, I quite fancied our chances. Incredibly, right at the start of the match, Cobblers began to dominate proceedings. Atkins really seemed to have instilled some new passion and quality into the side. After the success of the previous game against Colchester he decided to start with Neil Grayson down the middle with Jason White. Grayson looked fired up for it.

On fourteen minutes, some terrific work by Chris Burns set Neil Grayson away. Grayson drew goalkeeper John Vaughan off his line and slotted the ball into the corner of the net. What a start! I did not want to get too carried away at this point. There were still seventy-five minutes left on the clock and I could not help but remember who Preston had up front! I had mixed vibes before the game. They became better and better the longer the first half continued. The Cobblers' midfield of Peer, Hunter and Burns seemed in total command. We were lapping it up! For the last ten minutes or so of the half, Preston started to put on the pressure. Bennett came very close with a looping header. When the half-time whistle went though, Andy Woodman walked off knowing he had not had to make one save in anger.

The second half kicked off and at last the home supporters started to make some noise. This though did not last very long as Preston could find no way past Warburton and O'Shea. With twenty minutes left on the clock Preston won a corner. Thankfully it was cleared to White who broke forward with Grayson screaming down his left and Sampson coming down his right like a rocket. As White approached the Preston box he passed to Grayson who then passed one touch to Sampson who fired a shot towards goal. Vaughan at full stretch managed to get a hand down in time to stop a certain goal. Unluckily for him though, Grayson followed up the loose ball and within a split second his shot had the back of the net heaving. Moments like this you cannot describe. I was embracing Sharron, people around me were shouting and jumping up and down, John's eyes had become moist! Suddenly many Preston supporters could be seen leaving.

I could not relax though. Preston had scored heavily all season and with Bennett and Saville up front it was still far from over. Still though Woodman was not tested. Every cross that came over he plucked out of the air but they still failed to hit the target.

On seventy-seven minutes Cobblers won a free kick out by the far corner flag. Captain Ray Warburton came forward. The cross came over and Warburton connected with the ball and his header powered on to the underside of the bar. Many supporters felt then, and still do, that the ball crossed the line. In the confusion Preston failed to clear the ball under pressure from White. The ball broke free and who else but Neil Grayson turned and hammered in his second hat-trick of the season. A repeat scene happened only this time I found myself kissing Sharron! There was no way back for North End and it was only down to a finger tip save by Vaughan from a Jason White strike that it was not 4-0 two minutes from time. Whatever else is going on in the world at times like this fades into the distance. The sheer joy and pleasure on a few hundred people's faces inside that ground was proof enough of that. Wins of any sort are great, away ones especially, but to completely dominate against such a strong side who had only lost four league games in eight months was remarkable. Moments like that one at Preston do not happen very often.

We got back on board the coach for the trip back down to Sixfields. There were five coaches from Northampton at Preston that day. Big Dave was patrolling outside with a giant grin across his face. Many Cobblers' fans were punching the air, obviously on cloud nine. The police who I have to confess were excellent all afternoon, escorted us out and we headed for the M6. At this point we decided to watch the Shrewsbury v Cobblers 1993 video. The whole bus was roaring as Phil Chard and Pat Gavin twice, sunk Shrewsbury yet again. I'm convinced that video gets better every time I see it! Half way home there was just one job left for steward Jones. With two away games left in the season I had to take bookings for Chester and Wigan. With that completed Walsall had arrived and just another hour of the journey was left.

Four months on from this game, Cobblers' skipper Ray Warburton attended a Supporters Trust open forum at Sixfields. One of the many questions put to him was what was the best moment of the 1995/6 season? Without a shadow of a doubt the best moment for Warburton had come at half past four that afternoon at Deepdale. He had averted his eyes from the game for a second to notice loads of Preston supporters heading towards the exits. It had been a great moment for him and his team.

April 13 had been a great day, one I will always remember. I'm happy not to run the bus regularly but it had been a good experience and one I will do again if asked. Sometimes football seems like the oxygen of life. It can be the be all and end all of things. That is until you get days like April 14. Mid-morning I received a phone call. It was George's sister. Their mum, Mary Clark to whom this book is dedicated and whom I had got to know very well through my days of working in the Coop, had died that morning. It brought me down to earth with a bump. George, my long time friend was now without his mum. Yes, there are other things more important than football.

Jason White, White, White......

Northampton's season drew to an end. They could not have wished for a tougher run-in if they tried. Had Preston won against Northampton then they would have all but gained outright promotion. Cobblers well and truly ruined their party. If Atkins' men thought they could relax after that fine result at a ground that they had never won at, then they were wrong. Their next game was against Gillingham who had themselves gone top of the table after Cobblers' win at Deepdale. With one thousand seven hundred away fans packed into a full Sixfields, Gillingham needed to win to be assured of outright promotion to Division Two. This seemed on course when they took an early lead after Fortune-West, a £5000 signing from Stevenage Borough, scrambled in an opening goal. The Gills boasted the tightest defence in senior football in the country in 1995/6. Going into April, their goalkeeper, Jim Stannard, had only conceded eighteen goals. Their tight defence was also physical. This was very noticeable at Sixfields. I certainly noticed an off the ball incident after only ten seconds when one of Jason White's calf muscles received some attention from a fullback's studs! Gillingham's promotion party was also spoilt by Atkins' men. After White saw a goal bound shot come back off a post, Chris Burns equalised with a fierce volley on sixty-six minutes. In spite of sustained Cobblers pressure the game ended all square at 1-1.

Atkins' men had once again halted another club's celebrations in their tracks. It was noticeable that the past week had taken its toll on the Cobblers. Three days after the bruising encounter with Gillingham, Cobblers travelled away to Chester for a twice rearranged fixture. This was a real six pointer as Chester themselves were on the edge of the play-offs. In a dire game played in front of only one thousand six hundred and forty-seven spectators, four hundred odd from Northampton, Cobblers lost to an eighty-eighth minute header. With that, Northampton's slim outside chance of reaching the play-offs vanished into thin air.

It was a strange night in Chester. It was my first visit to the newish Deva stadium, ground number sixty. Considering how new it was, I felt that its appearance and finish was shoddy. The back of the away end is simply white washed breeze blocks. With both ends terraced, the total capacity is still a small six thousand. Chester could throw this back in my face and say that Sixfields only holds seven thousand six hundred. That would be fair enough but Sixfields is all-seater. Also that night in Chester there were only about twelve hundred home supporters present for a crunch match. The atmosphere was very quiet with little noise coming from the home end until they scored in the eighty-eighth minute. Then a little chorus of

"You're not singing anymore!"

sprung up! (Rather like Doncaster earlier on in the season.) Atkins later admitted that there were things he got wrong in the season. Personally I believe that this night in Chester was one of them. I reckon it would have been an ideal opportunity to rest one or two tired legs and blood some of the highly rated youngsters.

The final game of the season saw a trek up to the North West again, this time to Springfield Park, Wigan. Another crunch game, but not for the Cobblers. They could relax. The play-offs had gone and they were assured of eleventh spot, eighty-first in the league. For Wigan though, things were a lot different. A win against Cobblers would guarantee them a place in the play-offs. In their programme Wigan had listed details of tickets and fixture details in the event of this happening. Also before the game, a great deal had been made of the close friendship between the two respective managers. Atkins and Wigan's John Deehan were the best of friends. Come three o'clock though that was forgotten.

Because of Wigan's strong position and a possible trip to Wembley beckoning, the home attendance more than doubled its usual gate. Incredibly, in spite of Cobblers having little to play for, an estimated thousand away fans made the journey north. Immediately though Deehan's side threw everything at Warburton's defence. Early on in the season Wigan had been one of my favourites for promotion. Aided by strong financial backing they had strengthened their squad which included three Spanish Under-21s. Before the transfer deadline in March, Wigan paid £120,000 to Leicester City for David Lowe. On eleven minutes their pressure paid off as Leonard met a cross, beat Woodman to the ball and his header slid into an unguarded net. Woodman claimed he was impeded. I saw nothing wrong with the goal. The cross had been inch perfect. Wigan continued to press. It was not looking good for the Cobblers. The only way out for Atkins' team was surely that Wigan could not keep up the intense pressure and pace at the end of such a gruelling season. As the half progressed, Woodman made up for his error on the first goal. We may be talking about Third Division football here, but he pulled off an incredible reflex save from a powering header, again from Leonard. The ball looked like splitting the net as Woodman tipped it on to the bar and out for a corner, a save that would have graced the top flight anywhere in the world.

Not long after this moment of magic, O'Shea pumped a free kick up to Christian Lee, a youngster Atkins had brought in instead of Jason White who found himself on the subs' bench. Lee won the ball and flicked it on to Ian Sampson who fired past Farnworth. Cobblers were back in it against the run of play.

"You'll never make the play-offs," came our cry!
Sampson's goal took the wind out of Wigan's sails. As the second half progressed Cobblers came more and more into the game. With fifteen minutes left on the clock the fresh legs of Jason White came on for Lee up front. Lee had certainly impressed. I don't know which it was but White looked fired up or cheesed off with being left out. His long legs chased every snippet. White certainly had his critics earlier on in the season. On some occasions he seemed to look only half interested. Atkins persisted with him much to the annoyance of many fickle fans.

His low must have come in the cup tie at Oxford where he looked almost pedestrian. His critics' vocal condemnation of him reached a crescendo at the Manor Ground. It was soon after this game that reports circulated that Jason White in fact was not a lazy, half interested player. He suffers from asthma. Being married to an asthmatic, I know some of the problems he would suffer from. The Club and physio Dennis Casey were aware of this and started to design a warm-up routine for White. This meant that he did a light warm-up with Casey in the minutes leading up to kick-off. Just before the teams would come out, White would join them but not before he had used his inhalers.

Atkins' faith in White and Casey's warm-up routine paid off. In December, Jason White had suddenly hit form. His first goal in the 3-1 away win at Fulham was summed up on the "Endsleigh League Round Up" as

"A goal to grace the higher flights of the league."

Ray Warburton at Fulham, Dec 95

When White came off the bench at Springfield Park he had fifteen minutes to make a name for himself. With the season just three minutes from its end White added another goal to his tally. The revitalised Peer broke down the middle. Norton was fed out to the right. His deep cross was met by Grayson who headed back across the six yard box. With his back to goal and a defender on him like a leech, White with a split second of skill flicked the ball over the defender and past Farnworth into the back of the net. What another fantastic moment! A thousand of us went mad as White milked the applause. Newcastle may have their Shearers, United their Cantonas, Liverpool their Fowlers. Cobblers and a thousand or so of us couldn't give a stuff about them. We had our Jason White.

Within seconds of him milking his credit hundreds upon hundreds of Wigan supporters had left or were making their way towards the exit. With just over two and a half minutes of injury time played, the referee, who I have to confess appeared to be taken in by the antics of the Spaniards, sounded the final whistle. For the third time in a month Northampton had gone to a party and totally ruined it for the opposition. I have no grudge against Preston, Gillingham or Wigan, but I have no sympathy for them. For the previous four seasons my beloved club had been hung, drawn and quartered by everyone from Plymouth to Carlisle. Apart from the odd occasion like at Walsall in 1994, Cobblers had been humiliated time and time again. We had laid down and died at Crawley, many times at Scunthorpe and had our bones picked at Chesterfield. For all too long Northampton had been welcome at parties. The tide now appeared to be turning. They were becoming far from welcome!

Cobblers' win at Wigan left the season's total points at sixty-seven. Although they had only finished eleventh, Cobblers ended up only three points off a play-off place. They had won nine away games. They had beaten most of the top clubs, including a double over Bury who went on to gain outright promotion. Surprisingly, the Cobblers had struggled against teams near the foot of the table. They failed to beat bottom club Torquay, who survived the chop from the league because Stevenage's ground failed to meet the league deadline of December 31. In fact, Northampton never once got a hammering in 1995/6. The nearest they got to one was at Torquay when they lost 3-0. Take nothing away from Torquay's performance, but Cobblers were not helped by an extraordinary refereeing decision by Mr Wilkes. No I am not using the oldest excuse in the book and blaming the ref. With the score at 1-0, their goalkeeper Ashley Bayes handled outside the area with Jason White bearing down on him. An automatic red card like Woodman was to later get against Cardiff? Amazingly Bayes only got a yellow card. With no reserve goalkeeper on the bench, Bayes later pulled off a terrific save from a Chris Burns penalty and Torquay won 3-0 after scoring a last minute penalty. Later on in the season Mr Wilkes also refereed the Cobblers v Scunthorpe game at Sixfields. Late in the first half Roy Hunter was clear on goal, one on one with the goalkeeper. As he was about to strike the ball, Clarkson brought him down from behind. Penalty. To all and sundry present Clarkson had committed a professional foul. Mr Wilkes did not send him off. Burns again missed the penalty. In the second minute of the second half Clarkson scored for Scunthorpe who went on to win 2-1! No matter who you support decisions like this often puzzle and anger you. I'm sure that referees like Mr Wilkes give what they think to be correct at the time. Officials have a difficult job to do, one I would hate. Whereas I may have several hours to make a decision in my job, they have at most a second to make most of theirs. Having incidents like the one that happened to Bayes at Torquay is part and parcel of being a football supporter. At the time you will cry blue murder but when you look back at it things usually even themselves out and you would not change football for the world whether you support Cobblers, Falkirk or Arsenal.

The bus left Springfield Park on May 4 with Jim Tomlin, one of the stewards, dressed as Adolf Hitler for the day. Giving his salute to Wigan he uttered the words,

"Thank yoo for zee three points!"

The bus roared with laughter. It could have been the tension of the last five years coming out. In that time the fans had endured the Club all but going to the wall, the axing of the players, the fraught tension of Gay Meadow, the nightmare of Chesterfield, some awful displays in late 1994, culminating with that "Black Friday" against Scunthorpe, probably the worst performance I have ever seen. Atkins had been brought in as the new manager in January 1995. His only aim was to not let Northampton Town finish bottom of the entire league again. Days after he was appointed he attended a Trust meeting giving the fans present a very honest and truthful account of the limitations of the squad and how he hoped to improve it. Most of what he said that night had come true. He said it would take time and it had. His first game in charge bought three points and the Club ended up finishing seventeenth. Now a year later the roller-coaster ride of 1995/6 had finished. As the bus headed back down the M6 the expectation of the following season had already started. Finally at long last, Northampton Town had seemed to have turned the corner. There was a different tension now. One of expectation.

What Comes Naturally

Toilets

Before I draw this book to an end I thought that I must mention a problem faced by many supporters. Many football grounds are now being upgraded, either on their present sites or elsewhere at new complexes. Many of the old grounds are years behind in comfort and facilities. The way forward now is to redevelop but for many clubs this is a nigh on an impossibility. New stands or stadia do not come cheap. Even more worrying now is that with the National Lottery taking a large slice of the money and proceeds from the Pools companies, Football Trust money will also start to diminish. There will be even less money available to upgrade football stadia.

Northampton Town is fortunate. The Sixfields Stadium is the best thing that has ever happened to the Club. The facilities are tremendous. It was the first Football League stadium in the country to have disabled facilities on all four sides of the ground. It has become noticeable that the number of disabled supporters has increased enormously since the move away from the County Ground. Another tremendous feature of the stadium is that every seat in the ground can see all of the pitch. Not one seat is obstructed in any way. For once it seems that a Football Club is trying to treat ordinary supporters like human beings. In all fairness though, until October 1994, Northampton was stuck with one of the worst grounds in the league. The County Ground was a total embarrassment to the Club and its supporters.

The County Ground also boasted some of the worst toilets in the entire league, if not the world! I don't know what it is about football grounds but clubs seem to forget that supporters, like the rest of the human race and animal kingdom, need to perform bodily functions, such as urinating, pretty regularly. What I am about to write about is, I hope, a light-hearted way of describing how humans can be treated at football grounds. Although some of what follows may be funny, or some may think crude, it is a serious problem. What I describe at Swansea did actually happen. There are no reasons on this earth why people should be forced to suffer facilities, sometimes humiliations, like these. I'll start with the worst sight I have ever seen inside a football ground. In fact, it was probably one of the worst sights I have ever seen anywhere.

Swansea City.

The first time I visited the Vetch Field I was not overly impressed with the facilities. Swansea itself is an absolute nightmare to get to. The best way to get round the city is by foot. The entire centre seems to be blocked by an enormous traffic jam. If you ever go to see a game at Swansea always give yourself an extra hour to get there because you will almost certainly be sitting in a vehicle, probably within a mile and a half of the ground, going nowhere! This has happened every time I've been there.

The second time I visited the Vetch the same problem, only this time worse. On this occasion the approach into Swansea was at a total and utter standstill. I had the misfortune to have to drive to that game. I rarely go by car to away games. What is the point when there are cheap coaches run by the supporters clubs? This day though, for whatever reason, I had to drive. To cut a long story short the whole of Swansea, as usual, was bottlenecked. As three o'clock approached I was still some way off the ground, about half a mile. I made a detour and ended up in a private car park belonging to a well known hotel chain. Signs were up stating that any unauthorised parking would result in a fine. With kick-off just minutes off I made a decision, parked the car, hoped for the best and ran to the ground. Out of breath I finally arrived on the all but deserted terrace and looked at my watch. Seven minutes past three. Twenty-five minutes into the game the away end started to fill up. The coaches had arrived. Caught in the traffic as well!

By half-time I was bursting. I had not been since I left home. That season Swansea had decided to open up all of their away end. Previously, the left-hand side of the terrace had been fenced off. As a result this meant that there was another gents toilet in use. What better I thought. I could wander over, avoiding the usual crush, and empty my bladder in comparative peace. I strolled over and entered. I came to an

immediate stop as soon as I was confronted by what I saw. It was just about unbelievable and to this day I have never seen anything like it. The toilet itself was of average size. I cannot say anything else about it other than the entire toilet was just covered in several inches of stagnant, heaving urine with all sorts of bits and bobs floating on top. To put it politely, it was a lake of heaving urine. I literally ran out of there before I started to heave. I was just so pleased that I had managed to stop myself going any further otherwise I would have had very wet shoes, socks, trousers and feet. It does not bear thinking about. Looking on the bright side though, Cobblers managed a draw and I did not get a parking ticket.

The Hotel End toilet

96

Colchester United.

When the Cobblers play Colchester it is always billed as a local derby on television. In fact Colchester is nowhere near Northampton, it is a good two hours drive or if you are going on the train you have to go into London and back out again to get there. The only reason it could be called a local derby is that Northampton and Colchester are both in the Anglia and BBC East television regions. One is the furthest point west and the other is way out to the east. Even so, Cobblers always seem to take loads of supporters to Layer Road. Then as always the problems start.

The bottom line is that the ground is not designed for large away followings. When Cobblers travelled there in October 1995 there was a bigger than usual away following. I had been warned by a friend who had been there earlier in the season with Preston North End, that Layer Road had deteriorated. Preston had played at Colchester on a Tuesday night. In spite of the midweek fixture he said that North End had taken a good thousand fans down to Essex. The facilities just could not cope. There were three big problems. The view (appalling), refreshments (these ran out before kick-off) and worst of all the toilets, or rather the lack of them.

Two of these problems I thought would not affect me. One did not as I never eat food served up in football grounds. I have an extensive knowledge of the country's fish and chip shops. I usually frequent such an establishment or take my own pack ups. Surprisingly, in spite of my height, I did have problems with the view. The away end was heaving by kick-off and I was stuck at one end of this terrace with fencing, goal posts and roof supports in my line of vision. My Preston contact though was right: the toilets defied all belief. There must have been a thousand fans in the away end. For this we got two, yes two urinals and a lav, and the ladies were treated to just one toilet! I was very fortunate. I needed to go twenty minutes before kick-off. The queue was only six long then. John though could not wait. He nipped into the ladies which happened to be free. (There was a queue there when he had finished!) My bladder empty, I had no need to go back there that afternoon. A good job too, I hate to think what the queue was like at half-time!

The County Ground.

It has often been said that the County Ground was not in fact a football stadium but a car park for the county cricket club. As I have already said the ground was an embarrassment and one of, if not the worst ground in the Football League. There used to be a song sung on the Hotel End. It was called "I was born under the Hotel End". However there was one place under the Hotel End where you would not have wanted to be born, the gents lavatory. To walk past would be enough to knock you for six as the aroma enveloped your nostrils. Bad luck if at the time you were drinking a cup of tea or biting on your burger (although it was alleged that the County Ground burgers were in fact produced there). Walking past the gents lav under the Hotel End could have you reaching up against the wall at a split second's notice.

The problem with this urinal became more severe in the last two years of the Hotel End's life. This could have been because the new stadium was on the cards and the groundsman/cleaner just decided not to clean the place, if it was ever cleaned at all. The reason for this was apparent when you were forced to use it. There were two entrances to it. One though seemed to be permanently locked. This was probably because both the urinals were blocked at that end of the toilet. The result was that waste would build up in the urinal, with nowhere to go. Urggggggg. There was very little place for the waste to go. As the months ticked by, human waste was left in these urinals quicker than the blocked drains could clear it. For some games the problem would be so bad that much of the floor of the toilet would become very damp. If you did not know where the lav was, a trail of wet footprints would lead you to your destination!

In the summer things would change somewhat. Obviously with no football being played the toilet under the Hotel End would only be used by the occasional cricket spectator. This would mean that the blocked drains would gradually clear away some of the now, heaving wee. On really hot days in July the heat would evaporate much of the urine so that come the start of the new season of home matches in September the toilet would be dry. A mecca for rats. Utterly disgusting!

Mansfield.

When I was sitting down planning this chapter there was one toilet in the Football League that I just had to include although I was a bit worried as to how I was actually going to describe it. The reason for this is that I did not really see it, well I did but I didn't. Confused? Yes, so was I.

Mansfield until very recently was the largest town in Great Britain not to have a railway station. Mansfield is also the last Football League ground in the country with a toilet whose design allegedly goes back to the 70s, that's the 1870s! The last time I was at Mansfield was an utter nightmare. Northampton have a pretty good away following. Mansfield is one of our shorter journeys, about an hour and a half, so a larger than usual number of supporters regularly travel there. On that particular day, this was the case. Before kick-off I made my way to the gents to the side of the away terrace, or what's now left of it. After the coach journey up and a couple of pints I was ready to make use of the facilities. At that time I did not have any idea of the problems that not only would effect me, but all my fellow supporters as well.

I entered. The place was dark, cold and damp. Mansfield kindly and generously had supplied a light bulb to make things slightly more illuminating. This needed to be done as the bunker like toilet had very little light coming in and all the walls were painted black. Their generosity had not extended that far though. The light bulb was only forty watt! Just enough light to see in. I must stress the word, just. I thought nothing more about the toilet until the end of the game. For the record Cobblers lost 1-0. As it was deep mid-winter, darkness had descended over Mansfield as we trooped out to find our bus. I was walking past the toilet when I thought I better go just in case. Then the problems really started. As I approached the lav along with several other fans I started to walk inside. For whatever reason the light bulb was no longer working. With my hand on my heart I can say that it had almost certainly just conked out, rather than having been smashed. This was probably down to the very damp conditions. Electricity and moisture, as you will already know, do not mix.

I wandered in. The entire toilet was in complete darkness. As the game had just ended, the toilet was obviously busy. I had two choices. I could enter and just hope for the best or give up and try and wait until later. For me there was no second thought. The place was heaving with blokes. It was obviously crowded. The enormity of the problem was pretty worrying. How on earth anyone in this pit could possibly see where they were urinating still mystifies me to this day. Fortunately I was not desperate, so I waited until later.

I know I have tried to make this sound light-hearted but at the end of the day these are conditions which people should not be subjected to. If I had been so busting that I could not have waited, I may well have been forced to go outside, up against the terrace or out in the car park. What then would have happened? Would a steward or a policeman have escorted me down to the station and charged me with indecency? All through no fault of my own. Well done Mansfield. Marks out of ten, nought.

Scarborough

The McCain Stadium at Scarborough has undergone a big change since they entered the Football League. Both terraces behind the goals have been demolished to be replaced by new small all-seater stands. One thing though seems not to have been redeveloped. The gents toilet in the away end.

In 1994, Scarborough had just started to redevelop their ground. The home terrace on the east side of the ground was in the process of being demolished. All the home supporters therefore were congregated in a stand to our right. The away fans were out in the open on the west terrace. To our right, by the turnstiles were the toilets, both the gents and the ladies. Both teams were struggling in the league at this time (there's a surprise). When half-time came the score was not surprisingly 0-0. I wandered over to the gents to do what comes naturally. The toilets were in fact not too bad. The biggest problem was the size. There was room for two men to stand at the urinal and at the end of the lav was the toilet.

As I was waiting my turn two men were helping a lad out of his wheelchair so that he could use the toilet. As there was no room to swing a cat let alone position a wheelchair, it made me appreciate how lucky most of us are. To my way of thinking this lad was losing all dignity as a result of sheer short-sighted stupidity by Scarborough. Unfortunately they are not alone. I may be singling Scarborough out here but there are other clubs with facilities even worse. As you have already read, many able bodied people found it impossible to use the facilities at Mansfield.

When I had been, I wandered over to stand with Sharron and waited for the second half to start. She had a grin on her face.

"I could see you going for a leak," she said!

Sure enough, when I looked over to where the gents was, it had no door on the front! The bloke who was peeing into the urinal nearest the door had an audience, most of the away end!

In December 1995 Cobblers were once again playing at Scarborough. Again, Sharron and I had gone up to Whitby to stay for a long weekend. At this time the away terrace had also been demolished. Another new stand was going up. In spite of being moved alongside the pitch we entered the ground through the same turnstiles as the previous season. Sharron went in and I followed. As I went through the turnstile Sharron was in front of me putting her change into her purse. When this task had been completed she looked up to see where to go. Right in front of her and bang next door to the turnstile was the gents. It still had no door on it and it was very busy! She hurried along quickly. Some things had not changed at the McCain stadium.

Darlington 1994.

Each time I visit Darlo, the ground seems to get more and more run down. In late 1994 this was certainly the case.

For those of you who have not been to Darlo, the away end can only be described as appalling. As you entered it, you would have seen an old and battered caravan on your right-hand side. From the state of it and what it appeared to produce, I am sure that many away supporters had already decided to use it as a public convenience. I know this chapter is about toilets but where on earth did Darlo get this thing from? I mean, let's face it if a health inspector was to have taken one look at it they would think someone was taking the you know what. Another little thing about this Caravan/*hithouse/Refreshment Bar, how on earth did they ever get it into the ground? Those of you who have seen it and its position will know what I mean. It was totally enclosed within the ground in between the social club and the back of the away terrace.

Opposite the refreshment bar, tucked away behind the corner of the stand, could be found the lavatory. I use the word, lavatory quite liberally. On my third visit to Feathams I arrived at the ground early. Supporters were slowly trickling into the ground. After a pint of Strongarm in Richmond I was in need of a leak. I knew where to go. I nearly wet myself before I had entered the bog. As I turned into the gloomy entrance this young bird came flying out of the door! I stopped, took a deep breath and then entered. It is sometimes very important to compose yourself before venturing into such establishments. You just do not know what to expect.

Entering the gloom of the Darlo away end gents one could have been pleasantly surprised. Compared with other such locations it was very well lit. The light bulb must have been of the sixty watt variety. I concluded from this that Darlo's financial position must have been far better than that of Mansfield Town. Surprisingly there was a fair bit of room, unlike Colchester or Scarborough. Very quickly though things took a downward turn when it became apparent that the entire urinal was painted jet black. Even though the joint was exceptionally well lit with its single sixty watt bulb, one had to look very closely where one aimed. Light in dingy toilets does not reflect very well off black urinals. This can cause problems such as peeing over somebody or, even worse, slashing in their pocket which may contain their sandwiches! You may think this is silly talk, but remember the problems experienced at Mansfield!

The lav at Darlo

When I had carefully been, I thought I would check out the number two facilities. It became apparent from what I could see in the gloom that there was only one. Not a good sign when you may have people like myself that are addicted to vindaloo curry. As I peered through the door I was shocked to discover that the toilet seat was in place and secure. Unfortunately the entire thing was let down when I discovered that there was no toilet roll. I suppose I can understand why clubs do not put Andrex or Coop Economy Toilet Tissue in their lavs as somebody is always likely to nick it and throw it on to the pitch!

As I left the lav this young bird came back again and entered the lav. I watched as she made her way into a nest above the urinal. I suppose it was out of the elements and at least once a week it would be warmed up like a sauna. I never thought I would see a tit in the gents. I was right. It was a sparrow!

Darlington 1995

Twelve months later Cobblers returned to Feathams. Expecting the worst I came armed with my camera. As we entered the away end it became immediately apparent that Darlo had changed the refreshment bar. Gone was the caravan. Whether or not it had been removed or had actually fallen to bits I'll never know. In its place was a small posher looking trailer affair. Disappointed John and I made our way to the gents, whilst Sharron went next door into the ladies. Part of the bird's nest was still there in the corner. The urinals were still painted jet black. Darlo's financial position at this time had worsened. A forty watt light bulb now lit up the bunker. Worse was to follow though. John went to check the number two facilities out. Within a split second he was running out of the toilet reaching. I will not say any more, young people may be reading this. Sharron had an equally appalling time. Inside the ladies there was no water running. None whatsoever. Coupled with the non-flushing toilet there was only what seemed years old "Izal Medicated" paper available. Fortunately Sharron always carries a good supply of tissues on her. Utterly appalling, again.

At the end of the game Cobblers' fans were celebrating a rare 2-1 win at Feathams. We had to suffer the lav again. As we left the nightmare of a toilet somebody shouted,

"They haven't even got a Durex machine in there!"

***

Unfortunately these are not isolated incidents. Obviously being a male I have not really commented on the state of ladies lavs. From the outside they look no better than the gents loos. At Hereford in early 1995, John's wife Alison called him into the ladies just to witness what she had discovered. It was literally a concrete hole with no seat. Come on Hereford, you can do better than that, surely. Finally, before I finish this bit I must mention one other incident which totally sums up the inhumane way in which ordinary people can be treated at football grounds. Take a bow, Wrexham. On this day there were around three hundred Northampton fans in the away end. When the two coaches dropped us off outside the away end a quarter of an hour before kick-off, there was as usual a bee line towards the toilet. To cut a long story very short Wrexham's away end gents catered for about four blokes standing. There was a long queue! Some blokes were so desperate that they could not hold on. Many were forced to urinate up against the outside wall of the toilet. The facilities just could not cope. There was one problem with this. Very soon there was a stream of human waste heading towards the refreshment bar which Wrexham, in their wisdom, had situated yards from the toilet. Utterly appalling.

I have often wondered under what laws and rules football grounds come under? What would a health inspector have done if he had seen what I had seen heading towards the refreshment bar at Wrexham in October 1992? It's no joke.

Still Going Strong

Northampton Town are one hundred years old on 6 March 1997. There will be no telegram from Her Majesty but surely after the last five years the Cobblers deserve some sort of recognition. The Club are of course planning a series of events to mark this momentous occasion and hopefully put some much needed cash into the bank. I wonder how much publicity this will receive or whether it will fade into insignificance alongside the hype of the Premier League?

For supporters though life goes on. On average I reckon I miss half a dozen matches a season. This figure includes all Cobblers matches in the League, FA Cup, League Cup and Auto Windscreens Shield. It does not include reserve and pre-season friendlies. Personally speaking, I find pre-season friendlies pretty meaningless from a supporter's point of view, other than seeing new signings and how good they look. I have gone on record as saying that I believe the summer break from football is far too short. With the play-off finals finishing at the end of May and pre-season friendlies commencing around about the third week in July, that can leave less than a two month break for some clubs, their supporters and players.

I personally think that the football season should not start until September. As far as I am concerned August is still the cricket season and it can still be very hot in that month. I can see no pleasure in playing or even watching football when the temperature measured in the shade can soar well into the high eighties as it did on the opening day of the 1996/7 season. On this day I was playing cricket for Olney Town against Milton Keynes. Several players were totally shattered and dehydrated at the end of play. What on earth it must have felt like to chase round a football pitch in such conditions, I hate to think. By starting the new season in September, three weeks later than we do now would not automatically mean fixture congestion. By making the League Cup one leg instead of two would be an easy solution.

By stating that I only miss about six matches a season, I am not trying to make people think that I am some type of martyr. Far from it. Northampton Town have some supporters far more loyal than I will ever be. Of course as with any other club, there are far too many to mention but I feel I must single out just a few that I have come across. In the previous chapter you will have read about the time when John and I were approached at Exeter and asked to run the bus to Preston. You will have noted the name of Simon who was drinking at the bar with us. Following the Cobblers home and away you begin to recognise faces. There may be several hundred folk you will see on the terraces at Carlisle or Rochdale, but after a while many of these faces become familiar. I suppose it is rather like working for the company who presently employ me. In all there must be six hundred people on three different floors. After a while though you start to recognise faces. You may not know these people but they become familiar. Well Simon was one of these faces until Cobblers moved to Sixfields. John had bought his season ticket for the North Stand with my seat one row in front of his. Buying a season ticket in all-seater stadia can be a risky business. You never know who you may end up next to, behind or in front of for the rest of the season. You could have the misfortune to end up next to a so-called "supporter" like the one who used to stand to the right of the Hotel End goal.

"Wilcox you ******* *****r. What was that you ****?"

"Gleasure, just **** **f now. You could not even catch a cold."

Now these are not exaggerated comments. If anything I have moderated his vulgarity! They were common place. Could you imagine paying out a hundred and seventy pounds to listen to that type of rubbish for the rest of the season? You will always get one. The Hotel End heckler had the misfortune to stand behind me. In the end I could take no more and moved further up the terrace. In the North Stand you may not be so lucky. More often than not it sells out with you unable to move. Unlucky, you are well and truly stumped! Fortunately John was lucky and I suppose I was too come to that. From the first game at Sixfields until now Simon has taken his seat next to John. At that first game against Barnet, John and Simon recognised each other straightaway and fortunately have got on ever since. I suppose the relief went both ways! Not a surprise to know that we all retained the same seats for our season ticket.

When the Supporters Trust started running buses to away games, Simon decided to travel with us to some of the further venues. It was whilst on that evening trip to Exeter when Dave Linnell approached John and myself to run the bus up to Preston, that we learnt the full extent of Simon's dedication. It made me feel like a fair weather supporter. Needless to say he was reluctant to part with his incredible record when I asked him to confirm it for my book! Here is his record:

Last Cobblers game missed. 1 September 1990. Maidstone United away.
Last Cobblers home game missed. 21 April 1984. Doncaster Rovers.

Although Simon is fortunate to have a very good and understanding boss (himself!) what I find incredible is that he must have very good health! I can personally remember missing Gillingham away last season because of a very heavy cold. As I struggled to the front door I just knew that there was no way I was going to make the other side of it let alone Kent. As I struggled back into bed, the mercury inside the thermometer crept up over the arrow. Simon reckons he's just been lucky. My problem is that I have been stuck inside an air-conditioned building for nearly six years. As I finished writing this little piece on Simon, I learnt that he had managed to attend all eleven pre-season friendlies at the start of the 1996/7 campaign!

There is one group which I have hardly mentioned since the opening chapters of this book. What has happened to the Northampton Town Supporters Trust and their chairman, Brian Lomax since the heady days of 1992? At the start of the 1996/7 season the Trust is still going strong with a membership of five hundred and sixty. In the years and seasons since the McRitchie era, the Supporters Trust has maintained its presence on the Board of Directors of Northampton Town. Today the Trust has just one member on the Board of Directors and that is still Brian Lomax. The Supporters Trust is guaranteed a presence on the Board until 2019. This agreement was drawn up by the Borough Council on 26 July 1994 as part of the user agreement in respect of Sixfields Stadium.

Over the past five years I have got to know Brian Lomax pretty well, not just in his capacity of Chairman of the Trust but as a friend. Sometimes he has been left in some tricky situations. What a great many people forget is that in spite of being Chairman of the Trust and a Director of the Football Club, Brian Lomax is first and foremost a supporter of Northampton Town. Since those dark days of 1992 Brian has found himself on the receiving end of supporters' feelings. On the whole most of these feelings have been pleasant; on other occasions these feelings have turned hostile. Twice I have seen Brian vocally abused on the terraces at Darlington. I have seen him booed by a handful of people in the Hotel End. It is only human nature that you cannot please everybody. Being captain of one of Olney Town's league cricket teams don't I know that! Throughout the past five years though, Brian has always met the supporters head on. There have been times, like the occasion when Graham Carr was approached by the Northampton Board to become manager whilst Phil Chard was still actually in charge, that have angered lots of people. Brian has not hidden behind the curtain. He has met his hostile audience face to face. On the Carr incident he met them on a supporters coach to Lincoln City.

Ever since its formation in January 1992, the Trust has insisted on a democratic approach. As we know, this can be unusual in the world of football! After the traumatic months at the height of the McRitchie era, the Trust has insisted on carrying out its business in a way that is not really associated with the football set up. Since those days in 1992 when the then newly formed Trust decided to hold open public meetings to keep their members informed of events, this tradition has remained. The format is still the same and very simple. Brian Lomax will usually chair the meeting. At the front of the room with him will usually be an elected officer of the Trust. Normally this is the Secretary, Gareth Willsher. The Trust always invites special guests from the Club. It is not uncommon to see Ian Atkins addressing these open meetings. Directors of the Club have also been present along with several of the players, past and present. After the problems the Club experienced with the accounts back in 1992 the Trust has always adopted an open policy with its books. Its accounts are always open for any member to inspect.

Since its formation, the Northampton Town Supporters Trust has raised nearly £50,000. By the time this book has been published it should have exceeded that figure. Obviously in the early days fund-raising went very well. Collection buckets were a regular sight at the County Ground in early 1992. Below is a break down of what has been put into the Football Club:-

1992 - 93	£16835
1993 - 94	£15000
1994 - 95	£6485
1995 - 96	£4130
1996 - present	£5543

These figures may seem like chicken feed in comparison to the huge amounts of cash floating around the Premiership. In 1992 the Trust and the money it raised played a big part in Northampton Town's survival. The vast majority of the money raised has been pumped straight back into the Club. The first season of the "Trust Travel Club" in 1995/6 was also a success. From the outset the Travel Club has also gone down the same road as the Trust. It wanted to be accountable to its members. At the end of the season the Travel Club accounted for every penny they had received and spent. The final figure showed it had a surplus of income over expenditure of £3592. Obviously the main expenditure was the cost of hiring coaches but there were also a couple of interesting expenditure columns for everybody to see. The Travel Club gave Northampton Town £1138 towards the transfer fee of Ali Gibb. It also gave a further £587 to the Club in sponsorship. This may not seem like a lot of money to some people but in the Third Division it has meant the difference between signing a player or not.

In this final chapter I have singled out individuals and a couple of organisations for their dedication and unwavering support. Of course there are others who deserve to be chronicled such as two supporters, one from Exeter and the other from Crewe who follow Cobblers home and away. I should also mention a couple of individuals from Olney that I know like Fred Finch, who has had a season ticket at the Cobblers for as long as I can remember and an old chap who has seen practically every home game in the last sixty seasons! These are only the tip of the iceberg.

Of course Northampton Town are not the only club who have supporters who are very committed. Over the last year or so I have been working with a chap, Bruce Taylor, who supports Leyton Orient home and away. He has one slight draw back in his addiction. As he lives on the outskirts of Bletchley, every game he sees his side play is an away game for him. You will have seen the 3-0 Cobblers defeat at Torquay chronicled earlier in this book. Not long after this defeat Leyton Orient were playing at Plainmoor in the first round of the FA Cup. Bruce, of course made the long journey down to Devon. According to Bruce the game had not been a classic! The Os had been shocking and had been eliminated from the Cup thanks to a second half goal from Torquay. On the Monday morning at work, Bruce told us the full horror of his afternoon. Whilst Cobblers had just been put out by Oxford United, Bruce had been left totally distraught by one of the worse Leyton Orient displays he can ever remember. In fact, he was so frustrated and angered at what he had just witnessed that he found it totally impossible to drive home. He just sat in his car in Torquay and stewed. It was not until well over two hours after the final whistle that he had calmed down enough to turn the ignition on and head homewards. As we already know, Torquay is not just an hour's drive down the road! The trouble is though most of us can relate to Bruce's experience. Football gets you like that. Thankfully Bruce still follows Leyton Orient.

I calculated that in the last ten years I have travelled the equivalent of twice around the world to watch the Cobblers. I may not really have been born under the Hotel End, but I will, all being well, travel twice round the world again in the next ten years to support the claret and white. As I have said, people may think I'm mad for doing what I've done but I wouldn't change any of it.

I am obsessed.

The author would like to express his sincere thanks to the following people:-

Abraham Anstruther
John Thomas Brownlow
Andrew J Charter
Mark Chilton
John Clayton
Ian Cooper
Stephen Cooper
Stewart Farmer
Alan Frampton
Tony Galsworthy
Daniel Gibling
Maurice Hales B.E.M
Mike Horley
Sharron Jones
Mark Kennedy
Edwin R Lane
Chris Leleux
Tim Leleux
Brian Lomax
Franklin & Joy Loots (South Africa)
Michael 'Winnie' Loots
John Marlow
Peter J Martin (Jambo)
Thomas Moran
Mary Morrison
Simon Oliver
Keith Onley
Christopher Page
B J Parker
Tricia Picton
Christopher Prime
Edward Redmond
Chris Rowe
Peter Seaman
Pam Smithson
Robert Spick
Gary Talbot
Mike Taylor
Bruce Taylor
Dave Thorn
Gareth Viccars
David Walden
Peter Willett
Wicked Witch
Steve & Barbara Wright   (Derby County Supporters)